FINE
PRINTS

Titles on Science in Prometheus's Great Minds Series

See the back of this volume for a complete list of titles in
Prometheus's Great Books in Philosophy and Great Minds series.

FINGER PRINTS

FRANCIS GALTON

GREAT MINDS SERIES

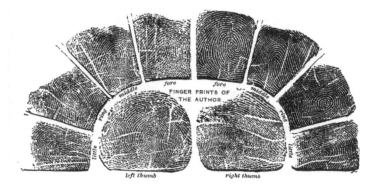

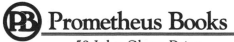 **Prometheus Books**

59 John Glenn Drive
Amherst, New York 14228-2197

Published 2006 by Prometheus Books

Inquiries should be addressed to
Prometheus Books
59 John Glenn Drive
Amherst, New York 14228–2197

716–691–0133 (x207). FAX: 716–564–2711.
WWW.PROMETHEUSBOOKS.COM

10 09 08 07 06   5 4 3 2 1

Library of Congress Cataloging-in-Publication Data

Galton, Francis, Sir, 1822–1911.
    Finger prints / Francis Galton.
        p. cm. (Great minds series)
    Originally published: London ; New York : Macmillan, 1892.
    Includes bibliographical references and index.
    ISBN-13: 978-1-59102-412-5
    ISBN-10: 1-59102-412-9
    (pbk. : alk paper) 1. Fingerprints—Identification. 2. Fingerprints—
Classification. I. Title. II. Series

GN192.G24 2006
599.9'45—dc22   2006008927

Printed in the United States of America on acid-free paper

S tatistician, world traveler, eugenicist, and pioneer in the use of fingerprints as a method of identification, SIR FRANCIS GALTON is best known for his investigations into heredity and human intelligence. Galton was born on February 16, 1822, in Sparkbrook, England, into a prominent Quaker family. His maternal grandfather was physician Erasmus Darwin, who penned a book that outlined his ideas of botany and generation. The youngest of seven children, Galton was also a cousin of Charles Darwin—a profound influence on Galton's scientific work.

Galton attended King Edward's School in the late 1830s and later pursued a medical career, at his family's insistence, first at King's College in London and later at Trinity College, Cambridge. Displeased with his choice of study, Galton switched to mathematics before falling ill, which, coupled with his father's serious health problems, rendered him unable to finish his degree. Following his father's death in 1844, the financially secure Galton began to travel abroad, initiating his scientific career with an excursion to Africa. Although unsuccessful in his attempt to find a southwest passage to Lake Ngami, situated north of the Kalahari Desert, Galton was elected a fellow of the Royal Geographical Society in 1853, the same year he married Louisa Jane Butler.

Six years later, Charles Darwin published his famous *Origin of the Species*, which reversed Galton's train of thought. Instead of thinking that all humans have essentially the same capabilities at birth, Galton now believed that heredity, not just the environment, played a role in shaping a person. In fact, Galton coined the phrase *nature versus nurture*, a concept still used today in the debate over the factors that influence human development.

Among the data that Galton gathered were collections of fingerprints. Galton demonstrated that, not only did fingerprint patterns remain the same on an individual from childhood through adulthood, but also each person has a unique set of prints, which can be used as a basis of identification. Interestingly, his work—an extension of William Herschel's proposal in the 1860s to identify criminals by their fingerprints and Dr. Henry Faulds's advocacy of the use of fingerprints in forensic work in 1880—ignited a decades-long feud between Herschel and Faulds. Galton, in collaboration with Sir Edward R. Henry, persuaded Scotland Yard to use fingerprints as a method of pinpointing lawbreakers in 1901.

He published a paper in 1888 and three books in the 1890s (including *Finger Prints* in 1892) on his work with fingerprint patterns.

Awards that Galton received are the Royal Society's Royal, Darwin, and Copley Medals (1876, 1902, and 1910, respectively); the Anthropological Institute's Huxley Medal (1901); and the Linnean Society's Darwin-Wallace Medal (1908). The British Association's general secretary between 1863 and 1867, Galton was knighted in 1909. In Surrey, England, Galton died on January 17, 1911.

Galton's bibliography remains incomplete because he wrote prolifically in a variety of publications, some well known and some obscure. Galton published at least 340 books and papers, some of which are still cited in current scientific articles. Books by Galton include *Tropical South Africa* (1853), *English Men of Science: Their Nature and Nurture* (1874), *Psychometric Facts* (1879), *Record of Family Faculties* (1884), and *Probability, the Foundation of Eugenics* (1907).

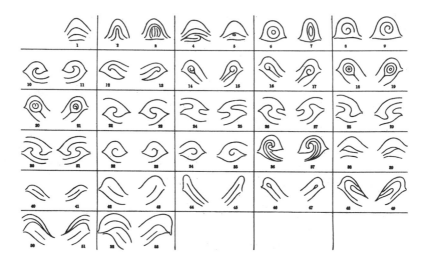

The "C" set of standard patterns for prints of the right hand.

CONTENTS

CHAPTER I

CHAPTER II

CHAPTER III

CHAPTER IV

CHAPTER V

CHAPTER VI

CHAPTER VII

CHAPTER VIII

CHAPTER IX

CHAPTER X

CHAPTER XI

CHAPTER XII

CHAPTER XIII

DESCRIPTION OF THE TABLES

XII. Index-headings under which more than 1 per cent of the sets were registered in 500 sets

XIII. Percentage of entries falling under a single head in 100, 300, and 500 sets

XIV. Number of different index-headings in 100 sets, according to the number of fingers in each set, and to the method of indexing

XV. Number of entries in 500 sets, each of the fore, middle, and ring-fingers only

XVI. Number of cases of various anthropometric data that severally fell in the three classes of large, medium, and small, when certain limiting values were adopted

XVII. Distribution of 500 sets of measures, each set consisting of five elements, into classes

XVIII. Number of the above sets that fell under the same headings

XIX. Further analysis of the two headings that contained the most numerous entries

XX. Observed random couplets

XXI. Calculated random couplets

XXII. Observed fraternal couplets

XXIII. Fraternal couplets—random, observed, and utmost feasible

XXIV. Three fingers of right hand in 150 fraternal couplets

XXV. Three fingers of right hand in 150 fraternal couplets—random and observed

XXVI. Three fingers of right hand in 150 fraternal couplets—resemblance measured on centesimal scale

XXVII. Twins

XXVIII. Children of like-patterned parents

XXIX. Paternal and maternal influence

XXX. Different races, percentage frequency of arches in fore-finger

XXXI. Distribution of number of ridges in AH, and of other measures in loops

XXXII. Ordinates to their schemes of distribution

XXXIII. Comparison of the above with calculated values

XXXIV. Proportions of a typical loop on the right and left thumbs, respectively

DESCRIPTION OF THE PLATES

I. Fig. 1. Chinese coin with the symbol of the nail-mark of the Empress Wen-teh

Fig. 2. Order on a camp sutler by Mr. Gilbert Thompson, who used his finger print for the same purpose as the scroll-work in cheques, viz., to ensure the detection of erasures

II. Fig. 3. Form of card used at my anthropometric laboratory for finger prints. It shows the places where they are severally impressed, whether dabbed or rolled (p. 47), and the hole by which they are secured in their box

Fig. 4. Small printing roller, used in the pocket apparatus, actual size. It may be covered either with india-rubber tubing or with roller composition

III. Fig. 5. Diagram of the chief peculiarities of ridges, called here *minutiæ* (the scale is about eight times the natural size)

Fig. 6. The systems of ridges and the creases in the palm, indicated respectively by continuous and by dotted lines. Nos. 2, 3, 4, and 5 show variations in the boundaries of the systems of ridges, and places where smaller systems are sometimes interpolated

IV. Fig. 7. The effects of scars and cuts on the ridges: *a* is the result of a deep ulcer; *b* the finger of a tailor (temporarily) scarred by the needle; *c* the result of a deep cut

Fig. 8. Formation of the interspace: filled in (3) by a loop; in (4)

by a scroll. The triangular plot or plots are indicated. In (1) there is no interspace, but a succession of arches are formed, gradually flattening into straight lines

V. Fig. 9. Specimens of rolled thumb prints, of the natural size, in which the patterns have been outlined, p. 70, and on which lines have been drawn for orientation and charting

VI. Fig. 10. Specimens of the outlines of the patterns on the ten digits of eight different persons, not selected but taken as they came. Its object is to give a general idea of the degree of their variety. The supply of ridges from the *inner* (or thumb side) are the darker ones, those from the *outer* are grey (the scale is of the natural size)

VII. Fig. 11. Standard patterns of Arches, together with some transitional forms, all with their names below

Fig. 12. As above, with respect to Loops

VIII. Fig. 13. As above, with respect to Whorls

Fig. 14. Cores to Loops, which may consist either of single lines, here called *rods*, or of a recurved line or *staple*, while the ridges that immediately envelops them is called an *envelope*

Fig. 15a. Cores to Whorls

IX. Fig. 15b. Transitional patterns, enlarged three times, between Arches and either Loops or Whorls

X. Fig. 16. Transitional patterns, as above, but between Loops and Whorls

XI. Fig. 17. Diagram showing the nine genera formed by the corresponding combinations of the two letters by which they are expressed, each being *i*, *j*, or *o* as the case may be. The first two diagrams are Arches, and not strictly patterns at all, but may with some justice be symbolised by *jj*

Fig. 18. Ambiguities in minutiæ, showing that certain details in them are not to be trusted, while others are

XII. Fig. 19. The illustrations to Purkenje's *Commentatio*. They are photo-lithographed from the original, which is not clearly printed

XIII. Fig. 20. Enlarged impressions of the same two fingers of V. H Hd., first when a child of 2½, and subsequently when a boy of 15 years of age. The lower pair are interesting from containing the unique case of failure of exact coincidence yet observed. It is marked A. The numerals indicate the correspondences

XIV. Fig. 21. Contains portions on an enlarged scale of eight couplets of finger prints, the first print in each couplet having been taken many years before the second, as shown by the attached dates. The points of correspondence in each couplet are indicated by similar numerals

XV. Fig. 22. The fore-finger of Sir W. J. Herschel as printed on two occasions, many years apart (enlarged scale). The numerals are here inserted on a plan that has the merit of clearness, but some of the lineations are thereby sacrificed

Fig. 23. Shows the periods of life over which the evidence of identity extends in Figs. 20–22.

CHAPTER I

INTRODUCTION

The palms of the hands and the soles of the feet are covered with two totally distinct classes of marks. The most conspicuous are the creases or folds of the skin which interest the followers of palmistry, but which are no more significant to others than the creases in old clothes; they show the lines of most frequent flexure, and nothing more. The least conspicuous marks, but the most numerous by far, are the so-called papillary ridges; they form the subject of the present book. If they had been only twice as large as they are, they would have attracted general attention and been commented on from the earliest times. Had Dean Swift known and thought of them, when writing about the Brobdingnags, whom he constructs on a scale twelve times as great as our own, he would certainly have made Gulliver express horror at the ribbed fingers of the giants who handled him. The ridges on their palms would have been as broad as the thongs of our coach-whips.

Let no one despise the ridges on account of their smallness, for they are in some respects the most important of all anthropological data. We shall see that they form patterns, considerable in size and of a curious variety of shape, whose boundaries can be firmly outlined, and which are little worlds in themselves. They have the unique merit of retaining all their peculiarities unchanged throughout life, and afford in consequence an incomparably surer criterion of identity than any other bodily feature. They may be made to throw welcome light on some of the most interesting biological questions of the day, such as heredity, symmetry, correlation, and the nature of genera and species. A representation of their lineations is easily secured in a self-recorded form, by inking the fingers in the way that will be explained, and pressing them on paper. There is no prejudice to be overcome in procuring these most trustworthy sign-manuals, no vanity to be pacified, no untruths to be guarded against.

My attention was first drawn to the ridges in 1888 when preparing a lecture on Personal Identification for the Royal Institution, which had for its principal object an account of the anthropometric method of Bertillon, then newly introduced into the prison administration of France. Wishing to treat the subject generally, and having a vague knowledge of the value sometimes assigned to finger marks, I made inquiries, and was surprised to find, both how much had been done, and how much there remained to do, before establishing their theoretical value and practical utility.

Enough was then seen to show that the subject was of real importance, and I resolved to investigate it; all the more so, as the modern processes of photographic printing would enable the evidence of such results as might be arrived at, to be presented to the reader on an enlarged and easily legible form, and in a trustworthy shape. Those that are put forward in the following pages, admit of considerable extension and improvement, and it is only the fact that an account of them seems useful, which causes me to delay no further before submitting what has thus far been attained, to the criticism of others.

I have already published the following memoirs upon this subject:

1. "Personal Identification." *Journal Royal Inst.* 25th May 1888, and *Nature*, 28th June 1888.

2. "Patterns in Thumb and Finger Marks." *Phil. Trans. Royal Society*, vol. clxxxii. (1891) b. pp. 1–23. [This almost wholly referred to thumb marks.]

3. "Method of Indexing Finger Marks." *Proc. Royal Society*, vol. xlix. (1891).

4. "Identification by Finger Tips." *Nineteenth Century*, August 1891.

This first and introductory chapter contains a brief and orderly summary of the contents of those that follow.

The second chapter treats of the previous employment of finger prints among various nations, which has been almost wholly confined to making daubs, without paying any regard to the delicate lineations with which this book is alone concerned. Their object was partly superstitious and partly ceremonial; superstitious, so far as a personal contact between the finger and the document was supposed to be of mysterious efficacy: ceremonial, as a formal act whose due performance in the presence of others could be attested. A few scattered instances are mentioned of persons who had made finger prints with enough care to show their lineations, and who had studied them; some few of these had used them as signatures. Attention is especially drawn to Sir William Herschel, who brought the method of finger prints into regular official employment when he was "Collector" or chief administrator of the Hooghly district in Bengal, and my large indebtedness to him is expressed in this chapter and in other places.

In the third chapter various methods of making good prints from the fingers are described at length, and more especially that which I have now adopted on a somewhat large scale, at my anthropometric laboratory, which, through the kindness of the authorities of South Kensington, is at present lodged in the galleries of their Science Collections. There, the ten digits of both hands of all the persons who come to be measured, are impressed with clearness and rapidity, and a very large collection of prints is steadily accumulating, each set being, as we shall see, a sign-manual that differentiates the person who made it, throughout the whole of his life, from all the rest of mankind.

Descriptions are also given of various methods of enlarging a finger print to a convenient size, when it is desired to examine it closely. Photography is the readiest of all; on the other hand the prism (as in a camera lucida) has merits of its own, and so has an enlarging pantagraph, when it is furnished with a small microscope and cross wires to serve as a pointer.

In the fourth chapter the character and purpose of the ridges, whose lineations appear in the finger print, are discussed. They have been the topic of a considerable amount of careful physiological study in late years, by writers who have investigated their development in early periods of unborn life, as well as their evolutionary history. They are perfectly defined in the monkeys, but appear in a much less advanced stage in other mammalia. Their courses run somewhat independently of the lines of flexure. They are studded with pores, which are the open mouths of ducts proceeding from the somewhat deeply-seated glands which secrete perspiration, so one of their functions is to facilitate the riddance of that excretion. The ridges increase in height as the skin is thickened by hard usage, until callosities begin to be formed, which may altogether hide them. But the way in which they assist the touch and may tend to neutralise the dulling effect of a thick protective skin, is still somewhat obscure. They certainly seem to help in the discrimination of the character of surfaces that are variously rubbed between the fingers.

These preliminary topics having been disposed of, we are free in the fifth chapter to enter upon the direct course of our inquiry, beginning with a discussion of the various patterns formed by the lineations. It will be shown how systems of parallel ridges sweep in bold curves across the palmar surface of the hand, and how, whenever the boundaries of two systems diverge, the interspace is filled up by a compact little system of its own, variously curved or whorled, having a fictitious resemblance to an eddy between two currents. An interspace of this kind is found in the bulb of each finger. The ridges run in parallel lines across the finger, up to its last joint, beyond which the insertion of the finger-nail causes a compression of the ridges on either side; their intermediate courses are in consequence so much broadened out that they commonly separate, and form two systems with an interspace between them. The independent patterns that appear in this interspace upon the bulbs of the fingers, are those with which this book is chiefly concerned.

At first sight, the maze formed by the minute lineations is bewildering, but it is shown that every interspace can be surely outlined, and when this is done, the character of the pattern it encloses, starts conspicuously into view. Examples are given to show how the outlining is performed, and others in which the outlines alone are taken into consideration. The cores of the patterns are also characteristic, and are described separately. It is they alone that have attracted the notice of previous inquirers. The outlines fall for the most part into nine distinct genera, defined by the relative directions of the divergent ridges that enclose them. The upper pair (those that run towards the finger-tip) may unite, or one or other of them may surmount the other, thus making three possibilities. There are three similar possibilities in respect to the lower pair; so, as any one of the first group may be combined with any one of the second, there are 3×3, or nine possibilities in all. The practice of somewhat rolling the finger when printing from it, is necessary in order to impress enough of its surface to ensure that the points at which the boundaries of the pattern begin to diverge, shall be always included.

Plates are given of the principal varieties of patterns, having regard only to their more fundamental differences, and names are attached for the convenience of description; specimens are also given of the outlines of the patterns in all the ten digits of eight different persons, taken at hazard, to afford a first idea of the character of the material to be dealt with. Another and less minute system of classification under three heads is then described, which is very useful for rough preliminary purposes, and of which frequent use is made further on. It is into Arches, Loops, and Whorls. In the Arches, there is no pattern strictly speaking, for there is no interspace; the need for it being avoided by a successive and regular broadening out of the ridges as they cross the bulb of the finger. In Loops, the interspace is filled with a system of ridges that bends back upon itself, and in which no one ridge turns through a complete circle. Whorls contain all cases in which at least one ridge turns through a complete circle, and they include certain double patterns which have a whorled appearance. The transitional cases are few; they are fully described, pictured, and classified. One great advantage of the rude A.L.W. system is that it can be applied, with little risk of error, to impressions that are smudged or imperfect; it is therefore very useful so far as it goes. Thus it can be easily applied to my own finger prints on the title-page, made as they are from digits that are creased and roughened by seventy years of life, and whose impressions have been closely clipped in order to fit them into a limited space.

A third method of classification is determined by the origin of the ridges which supply the interspace, whether it be from the thumb side or the little-finger side; in other words, from the Inner or the Outer side.

Lastly, a translation from the Latin is given of the famous Thesis or *Commentatio* of Purkenje, delivered at the University of Breslau in 1823, together with his illustrations. It is a very rare pamphlet, and has the great merit of having first drawn attention to the patterns and attempted to classify them.

In the sixth chapter we reach the question of Persistence: whether or no the patterns are so durable as to afford a sure basis for identification. The answer was different from what had been expected. So far as the proportions of the patterns go, they are *not* absolutely fixed, even in the adult, inasmuch as they change with the shape of the finger. If the finger is plumped out or emaciated, or variously deformed by usage, gout, or age, the proportions of the pattern will vary also. Two prints of the same finger, one taken before and the other after an interval of many years, cannot be expected to be as closely alike as two prints similarly made from the same woodcut. They are far from satisfying the shrewd test of the stereoscope, which shows if there has been an alteration even of a letter in two otherwise duplicate pages of print. The measurements vary at different periods, even in the adult, just as much if not more than his height, span, and the lengths of his several limbs. On the other hand, the numerous bifurcations, origins, islands, and enclosures in the ridges that compose the pattern, are proved to be *almost beyond change*. A comparison is made between the pattern on a finger, and one on a piece of lace; the latter may be stretched or shrunk as a whole, but the threads of which it is made retain their respective peculiarities. The evidence on which these conclusions are founded is considerable, and almost wholly derived from the collections made by Sir W. Herschel, who most kindly placed them at my disposal. They refer to one or more fingers, and in a few instances to the whole hand, of fifteen different persons. The intervals before and after which the prints were taken, amount in some cases to thirty years. Some of them reach from babyhood to boyhood, some from childhood to youth, some from youth to advanced middle age, one from middle life to incipient old age. These four stages nearly include the whole of the ordinary life of man. I have compared altogether some 700 points of reference in these couplets of impressions, and only found a single instance of discordance, in which a ridge that was cleft in a child became united in later years. Photographic enlargements are given in illustration, which include between them a total of 157 pairs of points of reference, all bearing distinctive numerals to facilitate comparison and to prove their unchangeableness. Reference is made to another illustrated publication of mine, which raises the total number of points compared to 389, all of which were successful, with the single exception above mentioned. The fact of an almost complete persistence in the peculiarities of the ridges from birth to death, may now be considered as determined. They existed before birth, and they persist after death, until effaced by decomposition.

In the seventh chapter an attempt is made to appraise the evidential value of finger prints by the common laws of Probability, paying great heed not to treat variations that are really correlated, as if they were independent. An artifice is used by which the number of portions is determined, into which a print may be divided, in each of which the purely local conditions introduce so much uncertainty, that a guess derived from a knowledge of the outside conditions is as likely as not to be wrong. A square of six ridge-intervals in the side was shown by three different sets of experiments to be larger than required; one of four ridge-intervals in the side was too small, but one of five ridge-intervals appeared to be closely correct. A six-ridge interval square was, however, at first adopted, in order to gain assurance that the error should be on the safe side. As an ordinary finger print contains about twenty-four of these squares, the uncertainty in respect to the entire contents of the pattern *due to this cause alone*, is expressed by a fraction of which the numerator is 1, and the denominator is 2 multiplied into itself twenty-four times, which amounts to a number so large that it requires eight figures to express it.

A further attempt was made to roughly appraise the neglected uncertainties relating to the outside conditions, but large as they are, they seem much inferior in their joint effect to the magnitude of that just discussed.

Next it was found possible, by the use of another artifice, to obtain some idea of the evidential value of identity when two prints agree in all but one, two, three, or any other number of particulars. This was done by using the five ridge-interval squares, of which thirty-five may be considered to go into a single finger print, being about the same as the number of the bifurcations, origins, and other points of comparison. The accidental similarity in their numbers enables us to treat them roughly as equivalent. On this basis the well-known method of binomial calculation is easily applied, with the general result that, notwithstanding a failure of evidence in a few points, as to the identity of two sets of prints, each, say, of three fingers, amply enough evidence would be supplied by the remainder to prevent any doubt that the two sets of prints were made by the same person. When a close correspondence exists in respect to all the ten digits, the thoroughness of the differentiation of each man from all the rest of the human species is multiplied to an extent far beyond the capacity of human imagination. There can be no doubt that the evidential value of identity afforded by prints of two or three of the fingers, is so great as to render it superfluous to seek confirmation from other sources.

The eighth chapter deals with the frequency with which the several kinds of patterns appear on the different digits of the same person, severally and in connection. The subject is a curious one, and the inquiry establishes unexpected relationships and distinctions between different fingers and between the two hands, to whose origin there is at present no clue. The relationships are themselves connected in the following way— calling any two digits on one of the hands by the letters A and B, respectively, and the digit on the other hand, that corresponds to B, by the symbol B1, then the kinship between A and B1. is identical, in a statistical sense, with the kinship between A and B.

The chief novelty in this chapter is an attempt to classify nearness of relationship upon a centesimal scale, in which the number of correspondences due to mere chance counts as 0°, and complete identity as 100°. It seems reasonable to adopt the scale with only slight reservation, when the average numbers of the Arches, Loops, and Whorls are respectively the same in the two kinds of digit which are compared together; but when they differ greatly, there are no means free from objection, of determining the 100° division of the scale; so the results, if noted at all, are subject to grave doubt.

Applying this scale, it appears that digits on opposite hands, which bear the same name, are more nearly related together than digits bearing different names, in about the proportion of three to two. It seems also, that of all the digits, none are so nearly related as the middle finger to the two adjacent ones.

In the ninth chapter, various methods of indexing are discussed and proposed, by which a set of finger prints may be so described by a few letters, that it can be easily searched for and found in any large collection, just as the name of a person is found in a directory. The procedure adopted, is to apply the Arch–Loop–Whorl classification to all ten digits, describing each digit in the order in which it is taken, by the letter *a*, *l*, or *w*, as the case may be, and arranging the results in alphabetical sequence. The downward direction of the slopes of loops on the fore-fingers is also taken into account, whether it be towards the Inner or the Outer side, thus replacing L on the fore-finger by either *i* or *o*.

Many alternative methods are examined, including both the recognition and the non-recognition of all sloped patterns. Also the gain in differentiation, when all the ten digits are catalogued, instead of only a few of them. There is so much correlation between the different fingers, and so much peculiarity in each, that theoretical notions of the value of different methods of classification are of little worth; it is only by actual trial that the best can be determined. Whatever plan of index be adopted, many patterns must fall under some few headings and few or no patterns under others, the former class resembling in that respect the Smiths, Browns, and other common names that occur in directories. The general value of the index much depends on the facility with which these frequent forms can be broken up by sub-classification, the rarer forms being easily dealt with. This branch of the subject has, however, been but lightly touched, under the belief that experience with larger collections than my own, was necessary before it could be treated thoroughly; means are, however, indicated for breaking up the large battalions, which have answered well thus far, and seem to admit of considerable extension. Thus, the number of ridges in a loop (which is by far the commonest pattern) on any particular finger, at the part of the impression where the ridges are cut by the axis of the loop, is a fairly definite and effective datum as well as a simple one; so also is the character of its inmost lineation, or core.

In the tenth chapter we come to a practical result of the inquiry, namely, its possible use as a means of differentiating a man from his fellows. In civil as well as in criminal cases, the need of some such system is shown to be greatly felt in many of our dependencies; where the features of natives are distinguished with difficulty; where there is but little variety of surnames; where there are strong motives for prevarication, especially connected with land-tenure and pensions, and a proverbial prevalence of unveracity.

It is also shown that the value to honest men of sure means of identifying themselves is not so small among civilised nations even in peace time, as to be disregarded, certainly not in times of war and of strict passports. But the value to honest men is always great of being able to identify offenders, whether they be merely deserters or formerly convicted criminals, and the method of finger prints is shown to be applicable to that purpose. For aid in searching the registers of a criminal intelligence bureau, its proper rank is probably a secondary one; the primary being some form of the already established Bertillon anthropometric method. Whatever power the latter gives of successfully searching registers, that power would be multiplied many hundredfold by the inclusion of finger prints, because their peculiarities are entirely unconnected with other personal characteristics, as we shall see further on. A brief account is given in this chapter of the Bertillon system, and an attempt is made on a small scale to verify its performance, by analysing five hundred sets of measures made at my own laboratory. These, combined with the quoted experiences in attempting to identify deserters in the United States, allow a high value to this method, though not so high as has been claimed for it, and show the importance of supplementary means. But whenever two suspected duplicates of measurements, bodily marks, photographs and finger prints have to be compared, the lineations of the finger prints would give an incomparably more trustworthy answer to the question, whether or no the suspicion of their referring to the same person was justified, than all the rest put together. Besides this, while measurements and photographs are serviceable only for adults, and even then under restrictions, the finger prints are available throughout life. It seems difficult to believe, now that their variety and persistence have been proved, the means of classifying them worked out, and the method of rapidly obtaining clear finger prints largely practised at my laboratory and elsewhere, that our criminal administration can long neglect the use of such a powerful auxiliary. It requires no higher skill and judgment to make, register, and hunt out finger prints, than is to be found in abundance among ordinary clerks. Of course some practice is required before facility can be gained in reading and recognising them, but not a few persons of whom I have knowledge, have interested themselves in doing so, and found no difficulty.

The eleventh chapter treats of Heredity, and affirmatively answers the question whether patterns are transmissible by descent. The inquiry proved more troublesome than was expected, on account of the great variety in patterns and the consequent rarity with which the same pattern, other than the common Loop, can be expected to appear in relatives. The available data having been attacked both by the Arch–Loop–Whorl method, and by a much more elaborate system of classification—described and figured as the C system, the resemblances between children of either sex, of the same parents (or more briefly "fraternal" resemblances, as they are here called, for want of a better term), have been tabulated and discussed. A batch of twins have also been analysed. Then cases have been treated in which both parents had the same pattern on corresponding fingers; this pattern was compared with the pattern on the corresponding finger of the child. In these and other ways, results were obtained, all testifying to the conspicuous effect of heredity, and giving results that can be measured on the centesimal scale already described. But though the qualitative results are clear, the quantitative are as yet not well defined, and that part of the inquiry must lie over until a future time, when I shall have more data and when certain foreseen improvements in the method of work may perhaps be carried out. There is a decided appearance, first observed by Mr. F. Howard Collins, of whom I shall again have to speak, of the influence of the mother being stronger than that of the father, in transmitting these patterns.

In the twelfth chapter we come to a branch of the subject of which I had great expectations, that have been falsified, namely, their use in indicating Race and Temperament. I thought that any hereditary peculiarities would almost of necessity vary in different races, and that so fundamental and enduring a feature as the finger markings must in some way be correlated with temperament.

The races I have chiefly examined are English, most of whom were of the upper and middle classes; the others chiefly from London board schools; Welsh, from the purest Welsh-speaking districts of South Wales; Jews from the large London schools, and Negroes from the territories of the Royal Niger Company. I have also a collection of Basque prints taken at Cambo, some twenty miles inland from Biarritz, which, although small, is large enough to warrant a provisional conclusion. As a first and only an approximately correct description, the English, Welsh, Jews, Negroes, and Basques, may all be spoken of as identical in the character of their finger prints; the same familiar patterns appearing in all of them with much the same degrees of frequency, the differences between groups of different races being not larger than those that occasionally occur between groups of the same race. The Jews have, however, a decidedly larger proportion of Whorled patterns than other races, and I should have been tempted to make an assertion about a peculiarity in the Negroes, had not one of their groups differed greatly from the rest. The task of examination has been laborious thus far, but it would be much more so to arrive with correctness at a second and closer approximation to the truth. It is doubtful at present whether it is worth while to pursue the subject, except in the case of the Hill tribes of India and a few other peculiarly diverse races, for the chance of discovering some characteristic and perhaps a more monkey-like pattern.

Considerable collections of prints of persons belonging to different classes have been analysed, such as students in science, and students in arts; farm labourers; men of much culture; and the lowest idiots in the London district (who are all sent to Darenth Asylum), but I do not, still as a first approximation, find any decided difference between their finger prints. The ridges of artists are certainly not more delicate and close than those of men of quite another stamp.

In Chapter XIII. the question is discussed and answered affirmatively, of the right of the nine fundamentally differing patterns to be considered as different genera; also of their more characteristic varieties to rank as different genera, or species, as the case may be. The chief test applied, respected the frequency with which the various Loops that occurred on the thumbs, were found to differ, in successive degrees of difference, from the central form of all of them; it was found to accord with the requirements of the well-known law of Frequency of Error, proving the existence of a central type, from which the departures were, in common phraseology, accidental. Now all the evidence in the last chapter concurs in showing that no sensible amount of correlation exists between any of the patterns on the one hand, and any of the bodily faculties or characteristics on the other. It would be absurd therefore to assert that in the struggle for existence, a person with, say, a loop on his right middle finger has a better chance of survival, or a better chance of early marriage, than one with an arch. Consequently genera and species are here seen to be formed without the slightest aid from either Natural or Sexual Selection, and these finger patterns are apparently the only peculiarity in which Panmixia, or the effect of promiscuous marriages, admits of being studied on a large scale. The result of Panmixia in finger markings, corroborates the arguments I have used in *Natural Inheritance* and elsewhere, to show that "organic stability" is the primary factor by which the distinctions between genera are maintained; consequently, the progress of evolution is not a smooth and uniform progression, but one that proceeds by jerks, through successive "sports" (as they are called), some of them implying considerable organic changes, and each in its turn being favoured by Natural Selection.

The same word "variation" has been indiscriminately applied to two very different conceptions, which ought to be clearly distinguished; the one is that of the "sports" just alluded to, which are changes in the position of organic stability, and may, through the aid of Natural Selection, become fresh steps in the onward course of evolution; the other is that of the Variations proper, which are merely strained conditions of a stable form of organisation, and not in any way an overthrow of them. Sports do not blend freely together; variations proper do so. Natural Selection acts upon variations proper, just as it does upon sports, by preserving the best to become parents, and eliminating the worst, but its action upon mere variations can, as I conceive, be of no permanent value to evolution, because there is a constant tendency in the offspring to "regress" towards the parental type. The amount and results of this tendency have been fully established in *Natural Inheritance*. It is there shown, that after a certain departure from the central typical form has been reached in any race, a further departure becomes impossible without the aid of these sports. In the successive generations of such a population, the average tendency of filial regression towards the racial centre must at length counterbalance the effects of filial dispersion; consequently the best of the produce cannot advance beyond the level already attained by the parents, the rest falling short of it in various degrees.

In concluding these introductory remarks, I have to perform the grateful duty of acknowledging my indebtedness to Mr. F. Howard Collins, who materially helped me during the past year. He undertook the numerous and tedious tabulations upon which the chapters on Heredity, and on Races and Classes, are founded, and he thoroughly revised nearly the whole of my MS., to the great advantage of the reader of this book.

Chapter II
Previous Use of Finger Prints

The employment of impressions of the hand or fingers to serve as sign-manuals will probably be found in every nation of importance, but the significance attached to them differs. It ranges from a mere superstition that personal contact is important, up to the conviction of which this book will furnish assurance, that when they are properly made, they are incomparably the most sure and unchanging of all forms of signature. The existence of the superstitious basis is easily noted in children and the uneducated; it occupies a prominent place in the witchcrafts of barbarians. The modern witness who swears on the Bible, is made to hold it and afterwards to kiss it; he who signs a document, touches a seal or wafer, and declares that "this is my act and deed." Students of the primitive customs of mankind find abundant instances of the belief, that personal contact communicates some mysterious essence from the thing touched to the person who touches it, and *vice versa;* but it is unnecessary here to enter further into these elementary human reasonings, which are fully described and discussed by various well-known writers.

The next grade of significance attached to an impression resembles that which commends itself to the mind of a hunter who is practised in tracking. He notices whether a footprint he happens to light upon, is larger or smaller, broader or narrower, or otherwise differs from the average, in any special peculiarity; he thence draws his inferences as to the individual who made it. So, when a chief presses his hand smeared with blood or grime, upon a clean surface, a mark is left in some degree characteristic of him. It may be that of a broad stumpy hand, or of a long thin one; it may be large or small; it may even show lines corresponding to the principal creases of the palm. Such hand prints have been made and repeated in many semi-civilised nations, and have even been impressed in vermilion on their State documents, as formerly by the sovereign of Japan. Though mere smudges, they serve in a slight degree to individualise the signer, while they are more or less clothed with the superstitious attributes of personal contact. So far as I can learn, no higher form of finger printing than this has ever existed, in regular and well-understood use, in any barbarous or semi-civilised nation. The ridges dealt with in this book could not be seen at all in such rude prints, much less could they be utilised as strictly distinctive features. It is possible that when impressions of the fingers have been made in wax, and used as seals to documents, they may sometimes have been subjected to minute scrutiny; but no account has yet reached me of trials in any of their courts of law, about disputed signatures, in which the identity of the party who was said to have signed with his finger print, had been established or disproved by comparing it with a print made by him then and there. The reader need be troubled with only a few examples, taken out of a considerable collection of extracts from books and letters, in which prints, or rather daubs of the above kind, are mentioned.

A good instance of their small real value may be seen in the *Trans. China Branch of the Royal Asiatic Society*, Part 1, 1847, published at Hong Kong, which contains a paper on "Land Tenure in China," by T. Meadows Taylor, with a deed concerning a sale of land, in facsimile, and its translation: this ends, "The mother and the son, the sellers, have in the presence of all the parties, received the price of the land in full, amounting to sixty-four taels and five mace, in perfect dollars weighed in scales. *Impression of the finger of the mother, of the maiden name of Chin.*" The impression, as it appears in the woodcut, is roundish in outline, and was therefore made by the tip and not the bulb of the finger. Its surface is somewhat mottled, but there is no trace of any ridges.

The native clerks of Bengal give the name of *tipsahi* to the mark impressed by illiterate persons who, refusing to make either a **X** or their caste-mark, dip their finger into the ink-pot and touch the document. The tipsahi is not supposed to individualise the signer, it is merely a personal ceremony performed in the presence of witnesses.

Many impressions of fingers are found on ancient pottery, as on Roman tiles; indeed the Latin word *palmatus* is said to mean an impression in soft clay, such as a mark upon a wall, stamped by a blow with the palm. Nail-marks are used ornamentally by potters of various nations. They exist on Assyrian bricks as signatures; for instance, in the Assyrian room of the British Museum, on the west side of the case C 43, one of these bricks contains a notice of sale and is prefaced by words that were translated for me thus: "Nail-mark of Nabu-sum-usur, the seller of the field, (used) like his seal." A somewhat amusing incident affected the design of the Chinese money during the great Tang dynasty, about 618 A.D. A new and important issue of coinage was to be introduced, and the Secretary of the Censors himself moulded the design in wax, and humbly submitted it to the Empress Wen-teh for approval. She, through maladroitness, dug the end of her enormously long finger-nail into its face, marking it deeply as with a carpenter's gouge. The poor Secretary of the Censors, Ngeu-yang-siun, who deserves honour from professional courtiers, suppressing such sentiments as he must have felt when his work was mauled, accepted the nail-mark of the Empress as an interesting supplement to the design; he changed it into a crescent in relief, and the new coins were stamped accordingly. (See *Coins and Medals*, edited by Stanley Lane Poole, 1885, p. 221.) A drawing of one of these is given in Plate 1, Fig. 1.

The European practitioners of palmistry and cheiromancy do not seem to have paid particular attention to the ridges with which we are concerned. A correspondent of the American journal *Science*, viii. 166, states, however, that the Chinese class the striæ at the ends of the fingers into "pots" when arranged in a coil, and into "hooks." They are also regarded by the cheiromantists in Japan. A curious account has reached me of negroes in the United States who, laying great stress on the possession of finger prints in wax or dough for witchcraft purposes, are also said to examine their striæ.

Leaving Purkenje to be spoken of in a later chapter, because he deals chiefly with classification, the first well-known person who appears to have studied the lineations of the ridges as a means of identification, was Bewick, who made an impression of his own thumb on a block of wood

FIG. 1.

Chinese Coin, Tang Dynasty, about 618 A.D., with nail mark of the Empress Wen-teh, figured in relief.

FIG. 2.

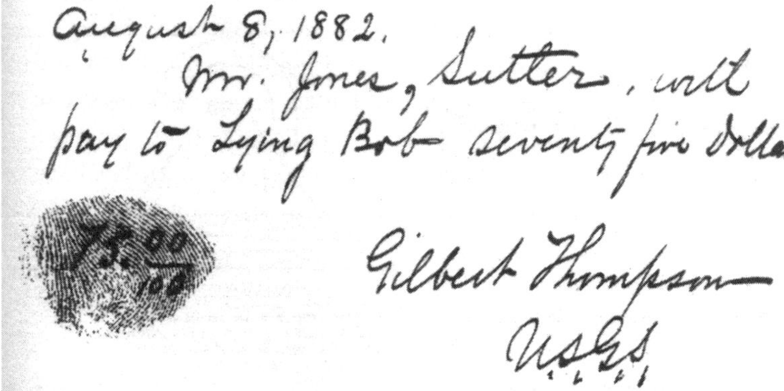

August 8, 1882.
Mr. Jones, Sutter, will pay to Lying Bob seventy five dollars,
Gilbert Thompson
U.S.G.S.

Order on a Camp Sutler, by the officer of a surveying party in New Mexico.   1882.

and engraved it, as well as an impression of a finger. They were used as fanciful designs for his illustrated books. Occasional instances of careful study may also be noted, such as that of Mr. Fauld (*Nature*, xxii. p. 605, Oct. 28, 1880), who seems to have taken much pains, and that of Mr. Tabor, the eminent photographer of San Francisco, who, noticing the lineations of a print that he had accidentally made with his own inked finger upon a blotting-paper, experimented further, and finally proposed the method of finger prints for the registration of Chinese, whose identificationhas always been a difficulty, and was giving a great deal of trouble at that particular time; but his proposal dropped through. Again Mr. Gilbert

Thompson, an American geologist, when on Government duty in 1882 in the wild parts of New Mexico, paid the members of his party by order of the camp sutler. To guard against forgery he signed his name across the impression made by his finger upon the order, after first pressing it on his office pad. He was good enough to send me the duplicate of one of these cheques made out in favour of a man who bore the ominous name of "Lying Bob" (Plate 1, Fig. 2). The impression took the place of the scroll work on an ordinary cheque; it was in violet aniline ink, and looked decidedly pretty. From time to time sporadic instances like these are met with, but none are comparable in importance to the regular and official employment made of finger prints by Sir William Herschel, during more than a quarter of a century in Bengal. I was exceedingly obliged to him for much valuable information when first commencing this study, and have been almost wholly indebted to his kindness for the materials used in this book for proving the persistence of the lineations throughout life.

Sir William Herschel has presented me with one of the two original "Contracts" in Bengali, dated 1858, which suggested to his mind the idea of using this method of identification. It was so difficult to obtain credence to the signatures of the natives, that he thought he would use the signature of the hand itself, chiefly with the intention of frightening the man who made it from afterwards denying his formal act; however, the impression proved so good that Sir W. Herschel became convinced that the same method might be further utilised. He finally introduced the use of finger prints in several departments at Hooghly in 1877, after seventeen years' experience of the value of the evidence they afforded. A too brief account of his work was given by him in *Nature*, xxiii. p. 23 (Nov. 25, 1880). He mentions there that he had been taking finger marks as sign-manuals for more than twenty years, and had introduced them for practical purposes in several ways in India with marked benefit. They rendered attempts to repudiate signatures quite hopeless. Finger prints were taken of Pensioners to prevent their personation by others after their death; they were used in the office for Registration of Deeds, and at a gaol where each prisoner had to sign with his finger. By comparing the prints of persons then living, with their prints taken twenty years previously, he considered he had proved that the lapse of at least that period made no change sufficient to affect the utility of the plan. He informs me that he submitted, in 1877, a report in semi-official form to the Inspector-General of Gaols, asking to be allowed to extend the process; but no result followed. In 1881, at the request of the Governor of the gaol at Greenwich (Sydney), he sent a description of the method, but no further steps appear to have been taken there.

If the use of finger prints ever becomes of general importance, Sir William Herschel must be regarded as the first who devised a feasible method for regular use, and afterwards officially adopted it. His method of printing for those purposes will be found in the next chapter.

CHAPTER III
METHODS OF PRINTING

It will be the aim of this chapter to show how to make really good and permanent impressions of the fingers. It is very easy to do so when the principles of the art are understood and practised, but difficult otherwise.

One example of the ease of making good, but not permanent impressions, is found, and should be tried, by pressing the bulb of a finger against well-polished glass, or against the highly-polished blade of a razor. The finger must be *very slightly* oiled, as by passing it through the hair; if it be moist, dry it with a handkerchief before the oiling. Then press the bulb of the finger on the glass or razor, as the case may be, and a beautiful impression will be left. The hardness of the glass or steel prevents its surface from rising into the furrows under the pressure of the ridges, while the layer of oil which covers the bottom of the furrows is too thin to reach down to the glass or steel; consequently the ridges alone are printed. There is no capillary or other action to spread the oil, so the impression remains distinct. A merely moist and not oily finger leaves a similar mark, but it soon evaporates.

This simple method is often convenient for quickly noting the character of a finger pattern. The impression may be made on a window-pane, a watch-glass, or even an eye-glass, if nothing better is at hand. The impression is not seen to its fullest advantage except by means of a single small source of bright light. The glass or steel has to be so inclined as just *not* to reflect the light into the eye. That part of the light which falls on the oily impression is not so sharply reflected from it as from the surface of the glass or steel. Consequently some stray beams of the light which is scattered from the oil, reach the eye, while all of the light reflected from the highly-polished glass or steel passes in another direction and is unseen. The result is a brilliantly luminous impression on a dark background. The impression ceases to be visible when the glass or steel is not well polished, and itself scatters the light, like the oil.

There are two diametrically opposed methods of printing, each being the complement of the other. The method used in ordinary printing, is to ink the projecting surfaces only, leaving the depressed parts clean. The other method, used in printing from engraved plates, is to ink the whole surface, and then to clean the ink from the projecting parts, leaving the depressions only filled with it. Either of these two courses can be adopted in taking finger prints, but not the two together, for when they are combined in equal degrees the result must be a plain black blot.

The following explanations will be almost entirely confined to the first method, namely, that of ordinary printing, as the second method has so far not given equally good results.

The ink used may be either printer's ink or water colour, but for producing the best work, rapidly and on a large scale, the method of printer's ink seems in every respect preferable. However, water colour suffices for some purposes, and as there is so much convenience in a pad, drenched with dye, such as is commonly used for hand stamps, and which is always ready for use, many may prefer it. The processes with printer's ink will be described first.

The relief formed by the ridges is low. In the fingers of very young children, and of some ladies whose hands are rarely submitted to rough usage, the ridges are exceptionally faint; their crests hardly rise above the furrows, yet it is the crests only that are to be inked. Consequently the layer of ink on the slab or pad on which the finger is pressed for the purpose of blackening it, must be *very thin*. Its thickness must be less than half the elevation of the ridges, for when the finger is pressed down, the crests displace the ink immediately below them, and drives it upwards into the furrows which would otherwise be choked with it.

It is no violent misuse of metaphor to compare the ridges to the crests of mountain ranges, and the depth of the blackening that they ought to receive, to that of the newly-fallen snow upon the mountain-tops in the early autumn, when it powders them from above downwards to a sharply-defined level. The most desirable blackening of the fingers corresponds to a snowfall which covers all the higher passes, but descends no lower.

With a finger so inked it is scarcely possible to fail in making a good imprint; the heaviest pressure cannot spoil it. The first desideratum is, then, to cover the slab by means of which the finger is to be blackened, with an extremely thin layer of ink.

This cannot be accomplished with printer's ink unless the slab is very clean, the ink somewhat fluid, and the roller that is used to spread it, in good condition. When a plate of glass is used for the slab, it is easy, by holding the inked slab between the eye and the light, to judge of the correct amount of inking. It should appear by no means black, but of a somewhat light brown.

The thickness of ink transferred by the finger to the paper is much less than that which lay upon the slab. The ink adheres to the slab as well as to the finger; when they are separated, only a portion of the ink is removed by the finger. Again, when the inked finger is pressed on the paper, only a portion of the ink that was on the finger is transferred to the paper. Owing to this double reduction, it seldom happens that a clear impression is at the same time black. An ideally perfect material for blackening would lie loosely on the slab like dust, it would cling very lightly to the finger, but adhere firmly to the paper.

The last preliminary to be noticed is the slowness with which the printer's ink hardens on the slab, and the rapidity with which it dries on paper. While serviceable for hours in the former case, in the latter it will be dry in a very few seconds. The drying or hardening of this oily ink has nothing whatever to do with the loss of moisture in the ordinary sense of the word, that is to say, of the loss of the contained water: it is wholly due to oxidisation of the oil. An extremely thin oxidised film soon forms on the surface of the layer on the slab, and this shields the lower-lying portions of the layer from the air, and retards further oxidisation. But paper is very unlike a polished slab; it is a fine felt, full of minute interstices. When a printed period (.) is placed under the microscope it looks like a drop of tar in the middle of a clean bird's-nest. The ink is minutely divided among the interstices of the paper, and a large surface being thereby exposed to the air, it oxidises at once, while a print from the finger upon glass will not dry for two or three days. One effect of oxidisation is to give a granulated appearance to the ink on rollers which have been allowed to get dirty. This granulation leaves clots on the slab which are fatal to good work: whenever they are seen, the roller must be cleaned at once.

The best ink for finger printing is not the best for ordinary printing. It is important to a commercial printer that his ink should dry rapidly on the paper, and he does not want a particularly thin layer of it; consequently, he prefers ink that contains various drying materials, such as litharge, which easily part with their oxygen. In finger prints this rapid drying is unnecessary, and the drying materials do harm by making the ink too stiff. The most serviceable ink for our purpose is made of any pure "drying" oil (or oil that oxidises rapidly), mixed with lampblack and very little else. I get mine in small collapsible tubes, each holding about a quarter of an ounce, from Messrs. Reeve & Sons, 113 Cheapside, London, W.C. Some thousands of fingers may be printed from the contents of one of these little tubes.

Let us now pass on to descriptions of printing apparatus. First, of that in regular use at my anthropometric laboratory at South Kensington, which has acted perfectly for three years; then of a similar but small apparatus convenient to carry about or send abroad, and of temporary arrangements in case any part of it may fail. Then lithographic printing will be noticed. In all these cases some kind of printer's ink has to be used. Next, smoke prints will be described, which at times are very serviceable; after this the methods of water colours and aniline dyes; then casts of various kinds; last of all, enlargements.

Laboratory apparatus. Mine consists of: 1, slab; 2, roller; 3, bottle of benzole (paraffin, turpentine, or solution of washing soda); 4, a funnel, with blotting-paper to act as a filter; 5, printer's ink; 6, rags and duster; 7, a small glass dish; 8, cards to print on.

The *Slab* is a sheet of polished copper, 10½ inches by 7, and about $\frac{1}{16}$ inch thick, mounted on a solid board ¾ inch thick, with projecting ears for ease of handling. The whole weighs 2½ lbs. Each day it is cleaned with the benzole and left bright. [A slab of more than double the length and less than half the width might, as my assistant thinks, answer better.]

The *Roller* is an ordinary small-sized printer's roller, 6 inches long and 3 in diameter, obtained from Messrs. Harrild, 25 Farringdon Street, London. Mine remained in good condition for quite a year and a half. When it is worn the maker exchanges it for a new one at a trifling cost. A good roller is of the highest importance; it affords the only means of spreading ink evenly and thinly, and with quickness and precision, over a large surface. The ingenuity of printers during more than four centuries in all civilised nations, has been directed to invent the most suitable composition for rollers, with the result that particular mixtures of glue, treacle, etc., are now in general use, the proportions between the ingredients differing according to the temperature at which the roller is intended to be used. The roller, like the slab, is cleansed with benzole every day (a very rapid process) and then put out of the reach of dust. Its clean surface is smooth and shining.

The *Benzole* is kept in a pint bottle. Sometimes paraffin or turpentine has been used instead; washing soda does not smell, but it dissolves the ink more slowly. They are otherwise nearly equally effective in cleansing the rollers and fingers. When dirty, the benzole can be rudely filtered and used again.

The *Funnel* holds blotting-paper for filtering the benzole. Where much printing is going on, and consequent washing of hands, it is worth while to use a filter, as it saves a little daily expense, though benzole is very cheap, and a few drops of it will clean a large surface.

The *Ink* has already been spoken of. The more fluid it is the better, so long as it does not "run." A thick ink cannot be so thinned by adding turpentine, etc., as to make it equal to ink that was originally fluid. The variety of oils used in making ink, and of the added materials, is endless. For our purpose, any oil that dries and does not spread, such as boiled or burnt linseed oil, mixed with lampblack, is almost all that is wanted. The burnt oil is the thicker of the two, and dries the faster. Unfortunately the two terms, burnt and boiled linseed oil, have no definite meaning in the trade, boiling or burning not being the simple processes these words express, but including an admixture of drying materials, which differ with each manufacturer; moreover, there are two, if not three, fundamentally distinct qualities of linseed, in respect to the oil extracted from it. The ink used in the laboratory and described above, answers all requirements. Many other inks have suited less well; less even than that which can be made, in a very homely way, with a little soot off a plate that had been smoked over a candle, mixed with such boiled linseed oil as can be bought at unpretentious oil and colour shops, its only fault being a tendency to run.

Rags, and a comparatively clean duster, are wanted for cleaning the slab and roller, without scratching them.

The small *Glass Dish* holds the benzole, into which the inked fingers are dipped before wiping them with the duster. Soap and water complete the preliminary cleansing.

Cards, lying flat, and being more easily manipulated than paper, are now used at the laboratory for receiving the impressions. They are of rather large size, 11½ × 5 inches, to enable the prints of the ten digits to be taken on the same card in two rather different ways (see Plate 2, Fig. 3), and to afford space for writing notes. The cards must have a smooth and yet slightly absorbent surface. If too highly glazed they cease to absorb, and more ink will remain on the fingers and less be transferred from them to the paper. A little trial soon determines the best specimen from among a few likely alternatives. "Correspondence cards" are suitable for taking prints of not more than three fingers, and are occasionally employed in the laboratory. Paper books and pads were tried, but their surfaces are inferior to cards in flatness, and their use is now abandoned.

The cards should be *very* white, because, if a photographic enlargement should at any time be desired, a slight tint on the card will be an impediment to making a photograph that shall be as sharp in its lines as an engraving, it being recollected that the cleanest prints are brown, and therefore not many shades darker than the tints of ordinary cards.

The method of printing at the laboratory is to squeeze a drop or so of ink on to the slab, and to work it thoroughly with the roller until a thin and even layer is spread, just as is done by printers, from one of whom a beginner might well purchase a lesson. The thickness of the layer of ink is tested from time to time by taking a print of a finger, and comparing its clearness and blackness with that of a standard print, hung up for the purpose close at hand. If too much ink has been put on the slab, some of it must be cleaned off, and the slab rolled afresh with what remains on it and on the roller. But this fault should seldom be committed; little ink should be put on at first, and more added little by little, until the required result is attained.

FIG. 3.

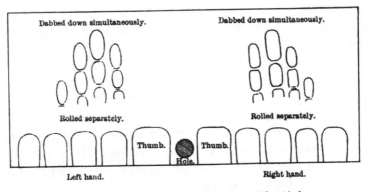

Form of card used for impressions of the ten digits. 11½ × 5 inches.

FIG. 4.

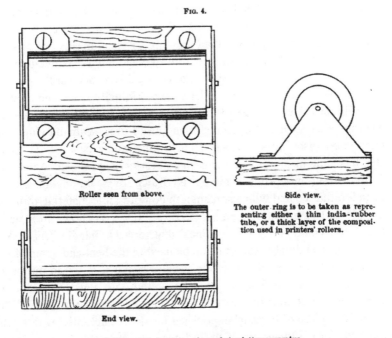

Roller seen from above.

End view.

Side view.

The outer ring is to be taken as representing either a thin india-rubber tube, or a thick layer of the composition used in printers' rollers.

Roller and its bearings, of a pocket printing apparatus.

The right hand of the subject, which should be quite passive, is taken by the operator, and the bulbs of his four fingers laid flat on the inked slab and pressed gently but firmly on it by the flattened hand of the operator. Then the inked fingers are laid flat upon the upper part of the right-hand side of the card (Plate 2, Fig. 3), and pressed down gently and firmly, just as before, by the flattened hand of the operator. This completes the process for one set of prints of the four fingers of the right hand. Then the bulb of the thumb is slightly *rolled* on the inked slab, and again on the lower part of the card, which gives a more extended but not quite so sharp an impression. Each of the four fingers of the same hand, in succession, is similarly rolled and impressed. This completes the process for the second set of prints of the digits of the right hand. Then the left hand is treated in the same way.

The result is indicated by the diagram, which shows on what parts of the card the impressions fall. Thus each of the four fingers is impressed twice, once above with a simple dab, and once below with a rolled impression, but each thumb is only impressed once; the thumbs being more troublesome to print from than fingers. Besides, the cards would have to be made even larger than they are, if two impressions of each thumb had to be included. It takes from two and a half to three minutes to obtain the eighteen impressions that are made on each card.

The *pocket apparatus* is similar to one originally made and used by Sir William J. Herschel (see Plate 2, Fig. 4, in which the roller and its bearings are drawn of the same size as those I use). A small cylinder of hard wood, or of brass tube, say 1¾ inch long, and ½ or ¾ inch in diameter, has a pin firmly driven into each end to serve as an axle. A piece of tightly-fitting india-rubber tubing is drawn over the cylinder. The cylinder, thus coated with a soft smooth compressible material, turns on its axle in two brackets, each secured by screws, as shown in Plate 2, Fig. 4, to a board (say 6 × 2½ × ¼ inch) that serves as handle. This makes a very fair and durable roller; it can be used in the heat and damp of the tropics, and is none the worse for a wetting, but it is by no means so good for delicate work as a cylinder covered with roller composition. These are not at all difficult to make; I have cast them for myself. The mould is a piece of brass tube, polished inside. A thick disc, with a central hole for the lower pin of the cylinder, fits smoothly into the lower end of the mould, and a ring with a thin bar across it, fits over the other end, the upper pin of the cylinder entering a hole in the middle of the bar; thus the cylinder is firmly held in the right position. After slightly oiling the inside of the mould, warming it, inserting the disc and cylinder, and fitting on the ring, the melted composition is poured in on either side of the bar. As it contracts on cooling, rather more must be poured in than at first appears necessary. Finally the roller is pushed out of the mould by a wooden ramrod, applied to the bottom of the disc. The composition must be melted like glue, in a vessel surrounded by hot water, which should never be allowed to boil; otherwise it will be spoilt. Harrild's best composition is more than twice the cost of that ordinarily used, and is expensive for large rollers, but for these miniature ones the cost is unimportant. The mould with which my first roller was made, was an old pewter squirt with the nozzle cut off; its piston served the double purpose of disc and ramrod.

The *Slab* is a piece of thick plate glass, of the same length and width as the handle to the roller, so they pack up easily together; its edges are ground to save the fingers and roller alike from being cut. (Porcelain takes the ink better than glass, but is not to be commonly found in the shops, of a convenient shape and size; a glazed tile makes a capital slab.) A collapsible tube of printer's ink, a few rags, and a phial of washing soda, complete the equipment (benzole may spoil india-rubber). When using the apparatus, spread a newspaper on the table to prevent accident, have other pieces of newspaper ready to clean the roller, and to remove any surplus of ink from it by the simple process of rolling it on the paper. Take care that the washing soda is in such a position that it cannot be upset and ruin the polish of the table. With these precautions, the apparatus may be used with cleanliness even in a drawing-room. The roller is of course laid on its back when not in use.

My assistant has taken good prints of the three first fingers of the right hands of more than 300 school children, say 1000 fingers, in a few hours during the same day, by this apparatus. Hawksley, 357 Oxford Street, W., sells a neatly fitted-up box with all the necessary apparatus.

Rougher arrangements. A small ball made by tying chamois leather round soft rags, may be used in the absence of a roller. The fingers are inked from the ball, over which the ink has been evenly distributed, by dabbing it many times against a slab or plate. This method gives good results, but is slow; it would be intolerably tedious to employ it on a large scale, on all ten digits of many persons.

It is often desirable to obtain finger prints from persons at a distance, who could not be expected to trouble themselves to acquire the art of printing for the purpose of making a single finger print. On these occasions I send folding-cases to them, each consisting of two pieces of thin copper sheeting, fastened side by side to a slip of pasteboard, by bending the edges of the copper over it. The pasteboard is half cut through at the back, along the space between the copper sheets, so that it can be folded like a reply post-card, the copper sheets being thus brought face to face, but prevented from touching by the margin of an interposed card, out of which the middle has been cut away. The two pieces of copper being inked and folded up, may then be sent by post. On arrival the ink is fresh, and the folders can be used as ordinary inked slabs. (See also Smoke Printing, page 53.)

The fluidity of even a very thin layer of ink seems to be retained for an indefinite time if the air is excluded to prevent oxidisation. I made experiments, and found that if pieces of glass (photographic quarter plates) be inked, and placed face to face, separated only by narrow paper margins, and then wrapped up without other precaution, they will remain good for a year and a half.

A slight film of oxidisation on the surface of the ink is a merit, not a harm; it is cleaner to work with and gives a blacker print, because the ink clings less tenaciously to the finger, consequently more of it is transferred to the paper.

If a blackened plate becomes dry, and is re-inked without first being cleaned, the new ink will rob the old of some of its oxygen and it will become dry in a day or even less.

Lithography. Prints may be made on "transfer-paper," and thence transferred to stone. It is better not to impress the fingers directly upon the stone, as the print from the stone would be reversed as compared with the original impression, and mistakes are likely to arise in consequence. The print is re-reversed, or put right, by impressing the fingers on transfer-paper. It might sometimes be desirable to obtain rapidly a large number of impressions of the finger prints of a suspected person. In this case lithography would be easier, quicker, and cheaper than photography.

Water Colours and Dyes. The pads most commonly used with office stamps are made of variously prepared gelatine, covered with fine silk to protect the surface, and saturated with an aniline dye. If the surface be touched, the finger is inked, and if the circumstances are all favourable, a good print may be made, but there is much liability to blot. The pad remains ready for use during many days without any attention, fresh ink being added at long intervals. The advantage of a dye over an ordinary water colour is, that it percolates the silk without any of its colour being kept back; while a solution of lampblack or Indian ink, consisting of particles of soot suspended in water, leaves all its black particles behind when it is carefully filtered; only clear water then passes through.

A serviceable pad may be made out of a few thicknesses of cloth or felt with fine silk or cambric stretched over it. The ink should be of a slowly drying sort, made, possibly, of ordinary ink, with the admixture of brown sugar, honey, glycerine or the like, to bring it to a proper consistence.

Mr. Gilbert Thompson's results by this process have already been mentioned. A similar process was employed for the Bengal finger prints by Sir W. Herschel, who sent me the following account: "As to the printing of the fingers themselves, no doubt practice makes perfect. But I took no pains with my native officials, some dozen or so of whom learnt to do it quite well enough for all practical purposes from Bengali written instructions, and using nothing but a kind of lampblack ink made by the native orderly for use with the office seal." A batch of these impressions, which he was so good as to send me, are all clear, and in most cases very good indeed. It would be easier to employ this method in a very damp climate than in England, where a very thin layer of lampblack is apt to dry too quickly on the fingers.

Printing as from Engraved Plates. Professor Ray Lankester kindly sent me his method of taking prints with water colours. "You take a watery brushful or two of the paint and rub it over the hands, rubbing one hand against the other until they feel sticky. A *thin* paper (tissue is best) placed on an oval cushion the shape of the hand, should be ready, and the hand pressed not too firmly on to it. I enclose a rough sample, done without a cushion. You require a cushion for the hollow of the hand, and the paint must be rubbed by the two hands until they feel sticky, not watery." This is the process of printing from engravings, the ink being removed from the ridges, and lying in the furrows. Blood can be used in the same way.

The following is extracted from an article by Dr. Louis Robinson in the *Nineteenth Century*, May 1892, p. 303—

> I found that direct prints of the infant's feet on paper would answer much better [than photography]. After trying various methods I found that the best results could be got by covering the foot by means of a soft stencil brush with a composition of lampblack, soap, syrup, and blue-black ink; wiping it gently from heel to toe with a smoothly-folded silk handkerchief to remove the superfluous pigment, and then applying a moderately flexible paper, supported on a soft pad, direct to the foot.

A curious method with paper and ordinary writing ink, lately contrived by Dr. Forgeot, is analogous to lithography. He has described in one of the many interesting pamphlets published by the "Laboratoire d'Anthropologie Criminelle" of Lyon (*Stenheil*, 2 Rue Casimir-Delavigne, Paris), his new process of rendering visible the previously invisible details of such faint finger prints as thieves may have left on anything they have handled, the object being to show how evidence may sometimes be obtained for their identification. It is well known that pressure of the hand on the polished surface of glass or metal leaves a latent image very difficult to destroy, and which may be rendered visible by suitable applications, but few probably have suspected that this may be the case, to a considerable degree, with ordinary paper. Dr. Forgeot has shown that if a slightly greasy hand, such for example as a hand that has just been passed through the hair, be pressed on clean paper, and if common ink be afterwards brushed lightly over the paper, it will refuse to lie thickly on the greasy parts, and that the result will be a very fair picture of the minute markings on the fingers. He has even used these productions as negatives, and printed good photographs from them. He has also sent me a photographic print made from a piece of glass which had been exposed to the vapour of hydrofluoric acid, after having been touched by a greasy hand. I have made many trials of his method with considerable success. It affords a way of obtaining serviceable impressions in the absence of better means. Dr. Forgeot's pamphlet describes other methods of a generally similar kind, which he has found to be less good than the above.

Smoke Printing. When other apparatus is not at hand, a method of obtaining very clear impressions is to smoke a plate over a lighted candle, to press the finger on the blackened surface, and then on an adhesive one. The following details must, however, be borne in mind: the plate must not be smoked too much, for the same reason that a slab must not be inked too much; and the adhesive surface must be only slightly damped, not wetted, or the impression will be blurred. A crockery plate is better than glass or metal, as the soot does not adhere to it so tightly, and it is less liable to crack. Professor Bowditch finds mica (which is sold at photographic stores in small sheets) to be the best material. Certainly the smoke comes wholly off the mica on to the parts of the finger that touch it, and a beautiful negative is left behind, which can be utilised in the camera better than glass that has been similarly treated; but it does not serve so well for a plate that is intended to be kept ready for use in a pocket-book, its softness rendering it too liable to be scratched. I prefer to keep a slip of very thin copper sheeting in my pocket-book, with which, and with the gummed back of a postage stamp, or even the gummed fringe to a sheet of stamps, impressions can easily be taken. The thin copper quickly cools, and a wax match supplies enough smoke. The folders spoken of (p. 49) may be smoked instead of being inked, and are in some cases preferable to carry in the pocket or to send by post, being so easy to smoke afresh. Luggage labels that are thickly gummed at the back furnish a good adhesive surface. The fault of gummed paper lies in the difficulty of damping it without its curling up. The gummed paper sold by stationers is usually thinner than luggage labels, and still more difficult to keep flat. Paste rubbed in a very thin layer over a card makes a surface that holds soot firmly, and one that will not stick to other surfaces if accidentally moistened. Glue, isinglass, size, and mucilage, are all suitable. It was my fortune as a boy to receive rudimentary lessons in drawing from a humble and rather grotesque master. He confided to me the discovery, which he claimed as his own, that pencil drawings could be fixed by licking them; and as I write these words, the image of his broad swab-like tongue performing the operation, and of his proud eyes gleaming over the drawing he was operating on, come vividly to remembrance. This reminiscence led me to try whether licking a piece of paper would give it a sufficiently adhesive surface. It did so. Nay, it led me a step further, for I took two pieces of paper and licked both.

The dry side of the one was held over the candle as an equivalent to a plate for collecting soot, being saved by the moisture at the back from igniting (it had to be licked two or three times during the process), and the impression was made on the other bit of paper. An ingenious person determined to succeed in obtaining the record of a finger impression, can hardly fail altogether under any ordinary circumstances.

Physiologists who are familiar with the revolving cylinder covered with highly-glazed paper, which is smoked, and then used for the purpose of recording the delicate movements of a tracer, will have noticed the beauty of the impression sometimes left by a finger that had accidentally touched it. They are also well versed in the art of varnishing such impressions to preserve them in a durable form.

A cake of blacklead (plumbago), such as is sold for blackening grates, when rubbed on paper leaves a powdery surface that readily blackens the fingers, and shows the ridges distinctly. A small part of the black comes off when the fingers are pressed on sticky paper, but I find it difficult to ensure good prints. The cakes are convenient to carry and cleanly to handle. Whitening, and still more, whitening mixed with size, may be used in the same way, but it gathers in the furrows, not on the ridges.

Casts give undoubtedly the most exact representation of the ridges, but they are difficult and unsatisfactory to examine, puzzling the eye by showing too conspicuously the variation of their heights, whereas we only want to know their courses. Again, as casts must be of a uniform colour, the finer lines are indistinctly seen except in a particular light. Lastly, they are both cumbrous to preserve and easily broken.

A sealing-wax impression is the simplest and best kind of cast, and the finger need not be burnt in making it. The plan is to make a considerable pool of flaming sealing-wax, stirring it well with the still unmelted piece of the stick, while it is burning. Then blow out the flame and wait a little, until the upper layer has cooled. Sealing-wax that has been well aflame takes a long time to harden thoroughly after it has parted with nearly all its heat. By selecting the proper moment after blowing out the flame, the wax will be cool enough for the finger to press it without discomfort, and it will still be sufficiently soft to take a sharp impression. Dentist's wax, which is far less brittle, is easily worked and takes impressions that are nearly as sharp as those of sealing-wax; it has to be well heated and kneaded, then plunged for a moment in cold water to chill the surface, and immediately impressed. Gutta-percha can also be used. The most delicate of all impressions is that left upon a thick clot of varnish, which has been exposed to the air long enough for a thin film to have formed over it. The impression is transient, but lingers sufficiently to be easily photographed. It happened, oddly enough, that a few days after I had noticed this effect, and had been experimenting upon it, I heard an interesting memoir "On the Minute Structure of Striped Muscle, with special allusion to a new method of investigation by means of 'Impressions' stamped in Collodion," submitted to the Royal Society by Dr. John Berry Haycraft, in which an analogous method was used to obtain impressions of delicate microscopic structures.

Photographs are valuable in themselves, and the negatives serve for subsequent *enlargements*. They are unquestionably accurate, and the labour of making them being mechanical, may be delegated. If the print be in printer's ink on white paper, the process is straightforward, first of obtaining a negative and afterwards photo-prints from it. The importance of the paper or card used to receive the finger print being quite white, has already been pointed out. An imprint on white crockery-ware is beautifully clear. Some of the photographs may be advantageously printed by the ferro-prussiate process. The paper used for it does not curl when dry, its texture is good for writing on, and the blue colour of the print makes handwriting clearly legible, whether it be in ink or in pencil.

Prints on glass have great merits for use as lantern slides, but it must be recollected that they may take some days to dry, and that when dry the ink can be only too easily detached from them by water, which insinuates itself between the dry ink and the glass. Of course they could be varnished, if the trouble and cost were no objection, and so preserved. The negative print left on an inked slab, after the finger has touched it, is sometimes very clear, that on smoked glass better, and on smoked mica the clearest of all. These have merely to be placed in the enlarging camera, where the negative image thrown on argento-bromide paper will yield a positive print. (See p. 92.)

I have made, by hand, many enlargements with a prism (camera lucida), but it is difficult to enlarge more than five times by means of it. So much shade is cast by the head that the prism can hardly be used at a less distance than 3 inches from the print, or one quarter the distance (12

FIG. 5.

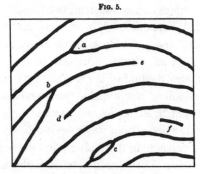

Characteristic peculiarities in Ridges
(about 8 times the natural size).

FIG. 6.

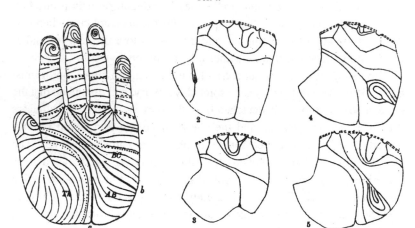

Systems of Ridges, and the Creases in the Palm.

inches) at which a book is usually read, while the paper on which the drawing is made cannot well be more than 15 inches below the prism; so it makes an enlargement of $^{4\times}\!\frac{5}{12}$ or five-fold. This is a very convenient method of analysing a pattern, since the lines follow only the axes of the ridges, as in Plate 3, Fig. 5. The prism and attached apparatus may be kept permanently mounted, ready for use at any time, without the trouble of any adjustment.

An enlarging pantagraph has also been of frequent use to me, in which the cross-wires of a low-power microscope took the place of the pointer. It has many merits, but its action was not equally free in all directions; the enlarged traces were consequently jagged, and required subsequent smoothing.

All hand-made enlargements are tedious to produce, as the total length of lineations to be followed is considerable. In a single finger print made by dabbing down the finger, their actual length amounts to about 18 inches; therefore in a five-fold enlargement of the entire print the pencil has to be carefully directed over five times that distance, or more than 7 feet.

Large copies of tracings made on transparent paper, either by the Camera Lucida or by the Pantagraph, are easily printed by the ferro-prussiate photographic process mentioned above, in the same way that plans are copied by engineers.

CHAPTER IV
THE RIDGES AND THEIR USES

The palmar surface of the hands and the soles of the feet, both in men and monkeys, are covered with minute ridges that bear a superficial resemblance to those made on sand by wind or flowing water. They form systems which run in bold sweeps, though the courses of the individual ridges are less regular. Each ridge (Plate 3, Fig. 5) is characterised by numerous minute peculiarities, called *Minutiæ* in this book, here dividing into two, and there uniting with another (*a, b*), or it may divide and almost immediately reunite, enclosing a small circular or elliptical space (*c*); at other times its beginning or end is markedly independent (*d, e*); lastly, the ridge may be so short as to form a small island (*f*).

Whenever an interspace is left between the boundaries of different systems of ridges, it is filled by a small system of its own, which will have some characteristic shape, and be called a *pattern* in this book.

There are three particularly well-marked systems of ridges in the palm of the hand marked in Plate 3, Fig. 6, 1, as Th, AB, and BC. The system Th is that which runs over the ball of the thumb and adjacent parts of the palm. It is bounded by the line *a* which starts from the middle of the palm close to the wrist, and sweeps thence round the ball of the thumb to the edge of the palm on the side of the thumb, which it reaches about half an inch, more or less, below the base of the fore-finger. The system AB is bounded towards the thumb by the above line *a*, and towards the little finger by the line *b*; the latter starts from about the middle of the little-finger side of the palm, and emerges on the opposite side just below the fore-finger. Consequently, every ridge that wholly crosses the palm is found in AB. The system BC is bounded thumbwards by the line *b*, until that line arrives at a point immediately below the axis of the fore-finger; there the boundary of BC leaves the line *b*, and skirts the base of the fore-finger until it reaches the interval which separates the fore and middle fingers. The upper boundary of BC is the line *c*, which leaves the little-finger side of the palm at a small distance below the base of the little finger, and terminates between the fore and middle fingers. Other systems are found between *c* and the middle, ring, and little fingers; they are somewhat more variable than those just described, as will be seen by comparing the five different palms shown in Fig. 6.

An interesting example of the interpolation of a small and independent system occurs frequently in the middle of one or other of the systems AB or BC, at the place where the space covered by the systems of ridges begins to broaden out very rapidly. There are two ways in which the necessary supply of ridges makes its appearance, the one is by a series of successive embranchments (Fig. 6, 1), the other is by the insertion of an independent system, as shown in 4, 5. Another example of an interpolated system, but of rarer occurrence, is found in the system Th, on the ball of the thumb, as seen in 2.

Far more definite in position, and complex in lineation, are the small independent systems which appear on the bulbs of the thumb and fingers. They are more instructive to study, more easy to classify, and will alone be discussed in this book.

In the diagram of the hand, Fig. 6, 1, the three chief cheiromantic creases are indicated by dots, but are not numbered. They are made (1) by the flexure of the thumb, (2) of the four fingers simultaneously, and (3) of the middle, ring, and little fingers simultaneously, while the fore-finger remains extended. There is no exact accordance between the courses of the creases and those of the adjacent ridges, less still do the former agree with the boundaries of the systems. The accordance is closest between the crease (1) and the ridges in Th; nevertheless that crease does not agree with the line *a*, but usually lies considerably within it. The crease (2) cuts the ridges on either side, at an angle of about 30 degrees. The crease (3) is usually parallel to the ridges between which it runs, but is often far from accordant with the line *c*. The creases at the various joints of the thumb and fingers cut the ridges at small angles, say, very roughly, of 15 degrees.

The supposition is therefore untenable that the courses of the ridges are wholly determined by the flexures. It appears, however, that the courses of the ridges and those of the lines of flexure may be in part, but in part only, due to the action of the same causes.

The fact of the creases of the hand being strongly marked in the newly-born child, has been considered by some to testify to the archaic and therefore important character of their origin. The crumpled condition of the hand of the infant, during some months before its birth, seems to me, however, quite sufficient to account for the creases.

I possess a few specimens of hand prints of persons taken when children, and again, after an interval of several years: they show a general accordance in respect to the creases, but not sufficiently close for identification.

The ridges on the feet and toes are less complex than those on the hands and digits, and are less serviceable for present purposes, though equally interesting to physiologists. Having given but little attention to them myself, they will not be again referred to.

The ridges are studded with minute pores which are the open mouths of the ducts of the somewhat deeply-seated glands, whose office is to secrete perspiration: Plate 10, n, is a good example of them. The distance between adjacent pores on the same ridge is, roughly speaking, about half that which separates the ridges. The lines of a pattern are such as an artist would draw, if dots had been made on a sheet of paper in positions corresponding to the several pores, and he endeavoured to connect them by evenly flowing curves; it would be difficult to draw a pattern under these conditions, and within definite boundaries, that cannot be matched in a living hand.

The embryological development of the ridges has been studied by many, but more especially by Dr. A. Kollmann,[1] whose careful investigations and bibliography should be consulted by physiologists interested in the subject. He conceives the ridges to be formed through lateral pressures between nascent structures.

---

1 *Der Tastapparat der Hand der menschlichen Rassen und der Affen.* Dr. Arthur Kollmann. Leopold Voss, Leipzig, 1883. He has also published a more recent memoir.

The ridges are said to be first discernible in the fourth month of fœtal life, and fully formed by the sixth. In babies and children the delicacy of the ridges is proportionate to the smallness of their stature. They grow simultaneously with the general growth of the body, and continue to be sharply defined until old age has set in, when an incipient disintegration of the texture of the skin spoils, and may largely obliterate them, as in the finger prints on the title-page. They develop most in hands that do a moderate amount of work, and they are strongly developed in the foot, which has the hard work ofsupporting the weight of the body. They are, as already mentioned, but faintly developed in the hands of ladies, rendered delicate by the continual use of gloves and lack of manual labour, and in idiots of the lowest type who are incapable of labouring at all. When the skin becomes thin, the ridges simultaneously subside in height. They are obliterated by the callosities formed on the hands of labourers and artisans in many trades, by the constant pressure of their peculiar tools. The ridges on the side of the left fore-finger of tailors and seamstresses are often temporarily destroyed by the needle; an instance of this is given in Plate 4, Fig. 7, b. Injuries, when they are sufficiently severe to leave permanent scars, destroy the ridges to that extent. If a piece of flesh is sliced off, or if an ulcer has eaten so deeply as to obliterate the perspiratory glands, a white cicatrix, without pores or ridges, is the result (Fig. 7, a). Lesser injuries are not permanent. My assistant happened to burn his finger rather sharply; the daily prints he took of it, illustrated the progress of healing in an interesting manner; finally the ridges were wholly restored. A deep clean cut leaves a permanent thin mark across the ridges (Fig. 7, c), sometimes without any accompanying puckering; but there is often a displacement of the ridges on both sides of it, exactly like a "fault" in stratified rocks. A cut, or other injury that is not a clean incision, leaves a scar with puckerings on all sides, as in Fig. 7, a, making the ridges at that part undecipherable, even if it does not wholly obliterate them.

The latest and best investigations on the evolution of the ridges have been made by Dr. H. Klaatsch.[1] He shows that the earliest appearance in the Mammalia of structures analogous to ridges is one in which small eminences occur on the ball of the foot, through which the sweat glands

---

1. "Morphologie der Tastballen der Saugethiere," *Jahrbuch*, xiv. p. 407. Leipzig, 1888.

FIG. 7.

SCARS AND CUTS, AND THEIR EFFECTS ON THE RIDGES.

a
Effect of an Ulcer.

b
Finger of a Tailor.

c
Effect of a Cut.

FIG. 8.

FORMATION OF INTERSPACE AND EXAMPLES OF THE ENCLOSED PATTERNS.

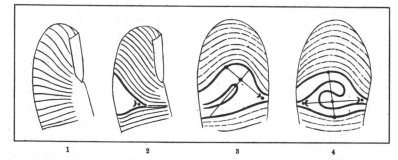

1   2   3   4

issue in no particular order. The arrangement of the papillæ into rows, and the accompanying orderly arrangement of the sweat glands, is a subsequent stage in evolution. The prehensile tail of the Howling Monkey serves as a fifth hand, and the naked concave part of the tail, with which it grasps and holds on to boughs, is furnished with ridges arranged transversely in beautiful order. The numerous drawings of the hands of monkeys by Allix[1] may be referred to with advantage.

The uses of the ridges are primarily, as I suppose, to raise the mouths of the ducts, so that the excretions which they pour out may the more easily be got rid of; and secondarily, in some obscure way, to assist the sense of touch. They are said to be moulded upon the subcutaneous papillæ in such a manner that the ultimate organs of touch, namely, the Pacinian bodies, etc.—into the variety of which it is unnecessary here to enter—are more closely congregated under the bases of the ridges than under the furrows, and it is easy, on those grounds, to make reasonable guesses how the ridges may assist the sense of touch. They must concentrate pressures, that would otherwise be spread over the surface generally, upon the parts which are most richly supplied with the terminations of nerves. By their means it would become possible to neutralise the otherwise dulling effect of a thick protective epidermis. Their existence in transverse ridges on the inner surface of the prehensile tails of monkeys admits of easy justification from this point of view. The ridges so disposed cannot prevent the tail from curling, and they must add materially to its sensitiveness. They seem to produce the latter effect on the hands of man, for, as the epidermis thickens under use within moderate limits, so the prominence of the ridges increases.

Supposing the ultimate organs of the sense of touch to be really congregated more thickly under the ridges than under the furrows—on which there has been some question—the power of tactile discrimination would depend very much on the closeness of the ridges. The well-known experiment with the two points of a pair of compasses, is exactly suited to test the truth of this. It consists in determining the smallest distance apart, of the two points, at which their simultaneous pressure conveys the sensation of a double prick. Those persons in whom the ridge-interval was short might be expected to perceive the double sensation,

---

1. *Ann. Sc. Nat.*, 5th series, vol. ix. 1868.

while others whose ridge-interval was wide would only perceive a single one, the distance apart of the compass points, and the parts touched by them, being the same in both cases. I was very glad to avail myself of the kind offer of Mr. E. B. Titchener to make an adequate course of experiments at Professor Wundt's psycho-physical laboratory at Leipzig, to decide this question. He had the advantage there of being able to operate on fellow-students who were themselves skilled in such lines of investigation, so while his own experience was a considerable safeguard against errors of method, that safety was reinforced by the fact that his experiments were conducted under the watchful eyes of competent and critical friends. The result of the enquiry was decisive. It was proved to demonstration that the fineness or coarseness of the ridges in different persons had no effect whatever on the delicacy of their tactile discrimination. Moreover, it made no difference in the results, whether one or both points of the compass rested on the ridges or in the furrows.

The width of the ridge-interval is certainly no test of the relative power of discrimination of the different parts of the same hand, because, while the ridge-interval is nearly uniform over the whole of the palmar surface, the least distance between the compass points that gives the sensation of doubleness is more than four times greater when they are applied to some parts of the palm than when they are applied to the bulbs of the fingers.

The ridges may subserve another purpose in the act of touch, namely, that of enabling the character of surfaces to be perceived by the act of rubbing them with the fingers. We all of us perform this, as it were, intuitively. It is interesting to ask a person who is ignorant of the real intention, to shut his eyes and to ascertain as well as he can by the sense of touch alone, the material of which any object is made that is afterwards put into his hands. He will be observed to explore it very carefully by rubbing its surface in many directions, and with many degrees of pressure. The ridges engage themselves with the roughness of the surface, and greatly help in calling forth the required sensation, which is that of a thrill; usually faint, but always to be perceived when the sensation is analysed, and which becomes very distinct when the indentations are at equal distances apart, as in a file or in velvet. A thrill is analogous to a musical note, and the characteristics to the sense of touch, of different surfaces when they are rubbed by the fingers, may be compared to different qualities of sound or noise. There are, however, no pure over-tones in the case of touch, as there are in nearly all sounds.

CHAPTER V
PATTERNS: THEIR OUTLINES AND CORES

The patterns on the thumb and fingers were first discussed at length by Purkenje in 1823, in a University Thesis or *Commentatio*. I have translated the part that chiefly concerns us, and appended it to this chapter together with his corresponding illustrations. Subsequent writers have adopted his standard types, diminishing or adding to their number as the case may be, and guided as he had been, by the superficial appearance of the lineations.

In my earlier trials some three years ago, an attempt at classification was made upon that same principle, when the experience gained was instructive. It had seemed best to limit them to the prints of a single digit, and the thumb was selected. I collected enough specimens to fill fourteen sheets, containing in the aggregate 504 prints of right thumbs, arranged in six lines and six columns ($6 \times 6 \times 14 = 504$), and another set of fourteen sheets containing the corresponding left thumbs. Then, for the greater convenience of study these sheets were photographed, and enlargements upon paper to about two and a half times the natural size made from the negatives. The enlargements of the right thumb prints were reversed, in order to make them comparable on equal terms with those of the left. The sheets were then cut up into rectangles about the size of small playing-cards, each of which contained a single print, and the register number in my catalogue was entered on its back, together with the letters L. for left, or R.R. for reversed right, as the case might be.

On trying to sort them according to Purkenje's standards, I failed completely, and many analogous plans were attempted without success. Next I endeavoured to sort the patterns into groups so that the central pattern of each group should differ by a unit of "equally discernible difference" from the central patterns of the adjacent groups, proposing to adopt those central patterns as standards of reference. After tedious re-sortings, some sixty standards were provisionally selected, and the whole laid by for a few days. On returning to the work with a fresh mind, it was painful to find how greatly my judgment had changed in the interim, and how faulty a classification that seemed tolerably good a week before, looked then. Moreover, I suffered the shame and humiliation of discovering that the identity of certain duplicates had been overlooked, and that one print had been mistaken for another. Repeated trials of the same kind made it certain that finality would never be reached by the path hitherto pursued.

On considering the causes of these doubts and blunders, different influences were found to produce them, any one of which was sufficient by itself to give rise to serious uncertainty. A complex pattern is capable of suggesting various readings, as the figuring on a wall-paper may suggest a variety of forms and faces to those who have such fancies. The number of illusive renderings of prints taken from the same finger, is greatly increased by such trifles as the relative breadths of their respective lineations and the differences in their depths of tint. The ridges themselves are soft in substance, and of various heights, so that a small difference in the pressure applied, or in the quantity of ink used, may considerably affect the width of the lines and the darkness of portions of the print. Certain ridges may thereby catch the attention at one time, though not at others, and give a bias to some false conception of the pattern. Again, it seldom happens that different impressions of the same digit are printed from exactly the same part of it, consequently the portion of the pattern that supplies the dominant character will often be quite different in the two prints. Hence the eye is apt to be deceived when it is guided merely by the general appearance. A third cause of error is still more serious; it is that patterns, especially those of a spiral form, may be apparently similar, yet fundamentally unlike, the unaided eye being frequently unable to analyse them and to discern real differences. Besides all this, the judgment is distracted by the mere size of the pattern, which catches the attention at once, and by other secondary matters such as the number of turns in the whorled patterns, and the relative dimensions of their different parts. The first need to be satisfied, before it could become possible to base the classification upon a more sure foundation than that of general appearance, was to establish a well-defined point or points of reference in the patterns. This was done by utilising the centres of the one or two triangular plots (see Plate 4, Fig. 8, 2, 3, 4) which are found in the great majority of patterns, and whose existence was pointed out by Purkenje, but not their more remote cause, which is as follows:

The ridges, as was shown in the diagram (Plate 3) of the palm of the hand, run athwart the fingers in rudely parallel lines up to the last joint, and if it were not for the finger-nail, would apparently continue parallel up to the extreme finger-tip. But the presence of the nail disturbs their parallelism and squeezes them downwards on both sides of the finger. (See Fig. 8, 2.) Consequently, the ridges that run close to the tip are greatly arched, those that successively follow are gradually less arched until, in some cases, all signs of the arch disappear at about the level of the first joint (Fig. 8, 1). Usually, however, this gradual transition from an arch to a straight line fails to be carried out, causing a break in the orderly sequence, and a consequent interspace (Fig. 8, 2). The topmost boundary of the interspace is formed by the lowermost arch, and its lower-most boundary by the topmost straight ridge. But an equally large number of ducts exist within the interspace, as are to be found in adjacent areas of equal size, whose mouths require to be supported and connected. This is effected by the interpolation of an independent system of ridges arranged in loops (Fig. 8, 3; also Plate 5, Fig. 9, a, f), or in scrolls (Fig. 8, 4; also Fig. 9, g, h), and this interpolated system forms the "pattern." Now the existence of an interspace implies the divergence of two previously adjacent ridges (Fig. 8, 2), in order to embrace it. Just in front of the place where the divergence begins, and before the sweep of the pattern is reached, there are usually one or more very short cross-ridges. Their effect is to complete the enclosure of the minute triangular plot in question. Where there is a plot on both sides of the finger, the line that connects them (Fig. 8, 4) serves as a base line whereby the pattern may be oriented, and the position of any point roughly charted. Where there is a plot on only one side of the finger (Fig. 8, 3), the pattern has almost nec-

FIG. 9.

EXAMPLES OF OUTLINED PATTERNS
(The Specimens are rolled impressions of natural size).

essarily an axis, which serves for orientation, and the pattern can still be charted, though on a different principle, by dropping a perpendicular from the plot on to the axis, in the way there shown.

These plots form corner-stones to my system of outlining and subsequent classification; it is therefore extremely important that a sufficient area of the finger should be printed to include them. This can always be done by slightly *rolling* the finger (p. 48), the result being, in the language of map-makers, a cylindrical projection of the finger (see Plate 5, Fig. 9, *a–h*). Large as these impressions look, they are of the natural size, taken from ordinary thumbs.

The outlines. The next step is to give a clear and definite shape to the pattern by drawing its outline (Fig. 9). Take a fine pen, pencil, or paint brush, and follow in succession each of the two diverging ridges that start from either plot. The course of each ridge must be followed with scrupulous conscientiousness, marking it with a clean line as far as it can be traced. If the ridge bifurcates, always follow the branch that trends towards the middle of the pattern. If it stops short, let the outline stop short also, and recommence on a fresh ridge, choosing that which to the best of the judgment prolongs the course of the one that stopped. These outlines have an extraordinary effect in making finger markings intelligible to an untrained eye. What seemed before to be a vague and bewildering maze of lineations over which the glance wandered distractedly, seeking in vain for a point on which to fix itself, now suddenly assumes the shape of a sharply-defined figure. Whatever difficulties may arise in classifying these figures, they are as nothing compared to those experienced in attempting to classify unoutlined patterns, the outlines giving a precision to their general features which was wanting before.

After a pattern has been treated in this way, there is no further occasion to pore minutely into the finger print, in order to classify it correctly, for the bold firm curves of the outline are even more distinct than the largest capital letters in the title-page of a book.

A fair idea of the way in which the patterns are distributed, is given by Plate 6. Eight persons were taken in the order in which they happened to present themselves, and Plate 6 shows the result. For greater clearness, shading has been employed to distinguish between the ridges that are supplied from the inner and outer sides of the hand, respectively. The words "right" and "left" *must be avoided* in speaking of patterns, for the two hands are symmetrically disposed, only in a reversed sense. The right hand does not look like a left hand, but like the reflection of a left hand in a looking-glass, and *vice versa*. The phrases we shall employ will be the *Inner* and the *Outer*; or thumb-side and little-finger side (terms which were unfortunately misplaced in my memoir in the *Phil. Trans.* 1891).

There need be no difficulty in remembering the meaning of these terms, if we bear in mind that the great toes are undoubtedly innermost; that if we walked on all fours as children do, and as our remote ancestors probably did, the thumbs also would be innermost, as is the case when the two hands are impressed side by side on paper. Inner and outer are better than thumb-side and little-finger side, because the latter cannot be applied to the thumbs and little fingers themselves. The anatomical words "radial" and "ulnar," referring to the two bones of the fore-arm, are not in popular use, and they might be similarly inappropriate, for it would sound oddly to speak of the radial side of the radius.

The two plots just described will therefore be henceforth designated as the Inner and the Outer plots, respectively, and symbolised by the letters I and O.

The system of ridges in Fig. 10 that comes from the inner side "I" are the darkest; those from the outer "O" are grey. The employment of shading instead of variously stippled surfaces is of conspicuous advantage to the great majority of persons.

It may be convenient when marking finger prints with letters for reference, to use those that look alike, both in a direct and in a reversed aspect, as they may require to be read either way. The print is a reversed picture of the pattern upon the digit that made it. The pattern on one hand is, as already said, a reversed picture of a similar pattern as it shows on the other. In the various processes by which prints are multiplied, the patterns may be reversed and re-reversed. Thus, if a finger is impressed on a lithographic stone, the impressions from that stone are reversals of the impression made by the same finger upon paper. If made on transfer paper and thence transferred to stone, there is a re-reversal. There are even more varied possibilities when photography is employed. It is worth recollecting that there are twelve capital letters in the English alphabet which, if printed in block type, are unaffected by being reversed. They are **A.H.I.M.O.T.U.V.W.X.Y.Z.** Some symbols do the same, such as,

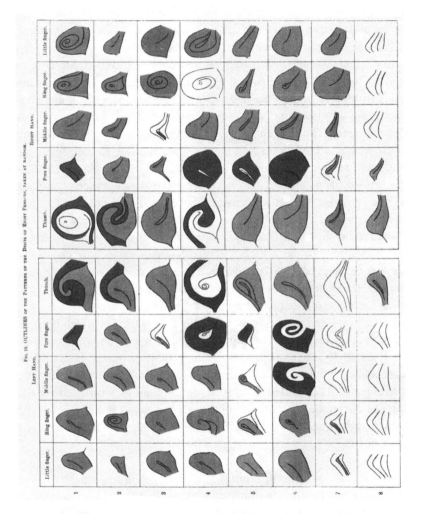

FIG. 10. OUTLINES OF THE PATTERNS OF THE DIGITS OF EIGHT PERSONS, TAKEN AT RANDOM.

*+ – = :. These and the letters **H.O.I.X.** have the further peculiarity of appearing unaltered when upside down.

Lenses. As a rule, only a small magnifying power is needed for drawing outlines, sufficient to allow the eye to be brought within six inches of the paper, for it is only at that short distance that the *minutiæ* of a full-sized finger print begin to be clearly discerned. Persons with normal sight, during their childhood and boy- or girlhood, are able to read as closely as this without using a lens, the range in adjustment of the focus of the eye being then large. But as age advances the range contracts, and an elderly person with otherwise normal eyesight requires glasses to read a book even at twelve inches from his eye. I now require much optical aid; when reading a book, spectacles of 12-inch focus are necessary; and when studying a finger print, 12-inch eye-glasses in addition, the double power enabling me to see clearly at a distance of only six inches. Perhaps the most convenient focus for a lens in ordinary use is 3 inches. It should be mounted at the end of a long arm that can easily be pushed in any direction, sideways, backwards, forwards, and up or down. It is undesirable to use a higher power than this unless it is necessary, because the field of view becomes narrowed to an inconvenient degree, and the nearer the head is to the paper, the darker is the shadow that it casts; there is also insufficient room for the use of a pencil.

Every now and then a closer inspection is wanted; for which purpose a doublet of ½-inch focus, standing on three slim legs, answers well.

For studying the markings on the fingers themselves, a small folding lens, sold at opticians' shops under the name of a "linen tester," is very convenient. It is so called because it was originally constructed for the purpose of counting the number of threads in a given space, in a sample of linen. It is equally well adapted for counting the number of ridges in a given space.

Whoever desires to occupy himself with finger prints, ought to give much time and practice to drawing outlines of different impressions of the same digits. His own ten fingers, and those of a few friends, will furnish the necessary variety of material on which to work. He should not rest satisfied until he has gained an assurance that all patterns possess definite figures, which may be latent but are potentially present, and that the ridges form something more than a nondescript congeries of ramifications and twists. He should continue to practise until he finds that the same ridges have been so nearly followed in duplicate impressions, that even in difficult cases his work will rarely vary more than a single ridge-interval.

When the triangular plot happens not to be visible, owing to the print failing to include it, which is often the case when the finger is not rolled, as is well shown in the prints of my own ten digits on the title-page, the trend of the ridges so far as they are seen, usually enables a practised eye to roughly estimate its true position. By means of this guidance an approximate, but fairly correct, outline can be drawn. When the habit of judging patterns by their outlines has become familiar, the eye will trace them for itself without caring to draw them, and will prefer an unoutlined pattern to work upon, but even then it is essential now and then to follow the outline with a fine point, say that of a penknife or a dry pen.

In selecting standard forms of patterns for the convenience of description, we must be content to disregard a great many of the more obvious characteristics. For instance, the size of generally similar patterns in Fig. 10 will be found to vary greatly, but the words large, medium, or small may be applied to any pattern, so there is no necessity to draw a standard outline for each size. Similarly as regards the inwards or outwards slope of patterns, it is needless to print here a separate standard outline for either slope, and equally unnecessary to print outlines in duplicate, with reversed titles, for the right and left hands, respectively. The phrase "a simple spiral" conveys a well-defined general idea, but there are four concrete forms of it (see bottom row of Plate 11, Fig. 17, *oj, jo, ij, ji*) which admit of being verbally distinguished. Again the internal proportions of any pattern, say, those of simple spirals, may vary greatly without affecting the fact of their being simple spirals. They may be wide or narrow at their mouths, they may be twisted up into a point (Plate 8, Fig. 14, 52), or they may run in broad curls of uniform width (Fig. 14, 51, 54). Perhaps the best general rule in selecting standard outlines, is to limit them to such as cannot be turned into any other by viewing them in an altered aspect, as upside down or from the back, or by magnifying or deforming them, whether it be through stretching, shrinking, or puckering any part of them. Subject to this general rule and to further and more par-

FIG. 11. ARCHES.

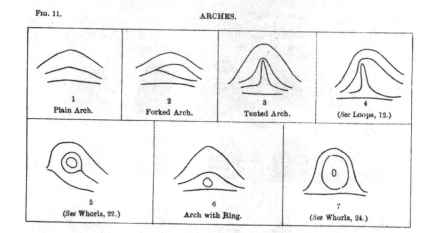

FIG. 12. LOOPS.

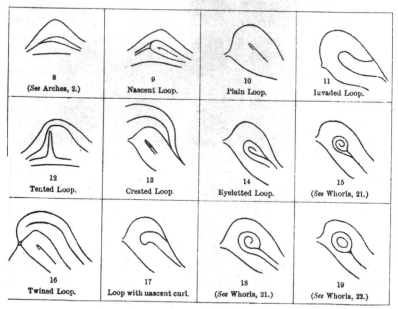

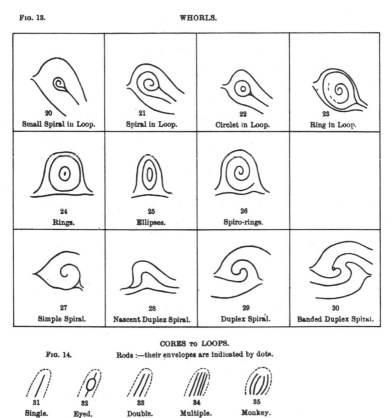

FIG. 13.   WHORLS.

| 20 Small Spiral in Loop. | 21 Spiral in Loop. | 22 Circlet in Loop. | 23 Ring in Loop. |

| 24 Rings. | 25 Ellipses. | 26 Spiro-rings. | |

| 27 Simple Spiral. | 28 Nascent Duplex Spiral. | 29 Duplex Spiral. | 30 Banded Duplex Spiral. |

CORES TO LOOPS.

FIG. 14.   Rods :—their envelopes are indicated by dots.

| 31 Single. | 32 Eyed. | 33 Double. | 34 Multiple. | 35 Monkey. |

Staples :—their envelopes are indicated by dots.

| 36 Plain. | 37 ¼ parted. | 38 ½ parted. | 39 ¾ parted. | 40 Tuning fork. | 41 Single eyed. | 42 Double eyed. |

Envelopes whether to Rods or Staples :—here staples only are dotted.

| 43 Plain. | 44 ¼ parted. | 45 ½ parted. | 46 ¾ parted. | 47 Single eyed. | 48 Double eyed. |

FIG. 15A.   CORES TO WHORLS.

| 49 Circles. | 50 Ellipses. | 51 Spiral. | 52 Twist. | 53 Plait. | 54 Deep Spiral. |

ticular descriptions, the sets (Plates 7 and 8, Figs. 11, 12, 13) will be found to give considerable help in naming the usual patterns.

It will be observed that they are grouped under the three principal heads of Arches, Loops, and Whorls, and that under each of these heads some analogous patterns as 4, 5, 7, 8, etc., are introduced and underlined with the word "see" so and so, and thus noted as really belonging to one of the other heads. This is done to indicate the character of the transitional cases that unite, respectively, the Arches with the Loops, the Arches with the Whorls, and the Loops with the Whorls. More will follow in respect to these. The "tented arch" (3) is extremely rare on the thumb; I do not remember ever to have seen it there, consequently it did not appear in the plate of patterns in the *Phil. Trans.* which referred to thumbs. On the other hand, the "banded duplex spiral" (30) is common in the thumb, but rare elsewhere. There are some compound patterns, especially the "spiral in loop" (21) and the "circlet in loop" (22), which are as much loops as whorls; but are reckoned as whorls. The "twinned loop" (16) is of more frequent occurrence than would be supposed from the examination of *dabbed* impressions, as the only part of the outer loop then in view resembles outside arches; it is due to a double separation of the ridges (Plate 4, Fig. 8), and a consequent double interspace. The "crested loop" (13) may sometimes be regarded as an incipient form of a "duplex spiral" (29).

The reader may also refer to Plate 16, which contains what is there called the C set of standard patterns. They were arranged and used for a special purpose, as described in Chapter XI. They refer to impressions of the right hand.

As a variety of Cores, differing in shape and size, may be found within each of the outlines, it is advisable to describe them separately. Plate 8, Fig. 14 shows a series of the cores of loops, in which the innermost lineations may be either straight or curved back; in the one case they are here called rods (31 to 35); in the other (36 to 42), staples. The first of the ridges that envelops the core, whether the core be a rod, many rods, or a staple, is also shown and named (43 to 48). None of the descriptions are intended to apply to more than the *very end* of the core, say, from the tip downwards to a distance equal to two average ridge-intervals in length. If more of the core be taken into account, the many varieties in their lower parts begin to make description confusing. In respect to the "parted" staples and envelopes, and those that are single-eyed, the description may further mention the side on which the parting or the eye occurs, whether it be the Inner or the Outer.

At the bottom of Fig. 14, 49–54, is given a series of rings, spirals, and plaits, in which nearly all the clearly distinguishable varieties are included, no regard being paid to the direction of the twist or to the number of turns. 49 is a set of concentric circles, 50 of ellipses: they are rarely so in a strict sense throughout the pattern, usually breaking away into a more or less spiriform arrangement as in 51. A curious optical effect is connected with the circular forms, which becomes almost annoying when many specimens are examined in succession. They seem to be cones standing bodily out from the paper. This singular appearance becomes still more marked when they are viewed with only one eye; no stereoscopic guidance then correcting the illusion of their being contour lines.

Another curious effect is seen in 53, which has the appearance of a plait or overlap; two systems of ridges that roll together, end bluntly, the end of the one system running right into a hollow curve of the other, and there stopping short; it seems, at the first glance, to run beneath it, as if it were a plait. This mode of ending forms a singular contrast to that shown in 51 and 52, where the ridges twist themselves into a point. 54 is a deep spiral, sometimes having a large core filled with upright and nearly parallel lines; occasionally they are bulbous, and resemble the commoner "monkey" type, see 35.

When the direction of twist is described, the language must be unambiguous: the following are the rules I adopt. The course of the ridge is always followed *towards* the *centre* of the pattern, and not away from it. Again, the direction of its course when so followed is specified at the place where it attains its *highest* point, or that nearest to the fingertip; its course at that point must needs be horizontal, and therefore directed either towards the inner or the outer side.

The amount of twist has a strong tendency to coincide with either one, two, three, four, or more half-turns, and not to stop short in intermediate positions. Here are indications of some unknown fundamental law, analogous apparently to that which causes Loops to be by far the commonest pattern.

The classification into Arches, Loops, and Whorls is based on the degree of curvature of the ridges, and enables almost any pattern to be sorted under one or other of those three heads. There are a few ambiguous patterns, and others which are nondescript, but the former are uncommon and the latter rare; as these exceptions give little real inconvenience, the classification works easily and well.

Arches are formed when the ridges run from one side to the other of the bulb of the digit without making any backward turn or twist. Loops, when there is a single backward turn, but no twist. Whorls, when there is a turn through at least one complete circle; they are also considered to include all duplex spirals.

The chief theoretical objection to this threefold system of classification lies in the existence of certain compound patterns, by far the most common of which are Whorls enclosed within Loops (Plates 7, 8, Fig. 12, 15, 18, 19, and Fig. 13, 20–23). They are as much Loops as Whorls, and properly ought to be relegated to a fourth class. I have not done so, but called them Whorls, for a practical reason which is cogent. In an imperfect impression, such as is made by merely dabbing the inked finger upon paper, the enveloping loop is often too incompletely printed to enable its existence to be surely ascertained, especially when the enclosed whorl is so large (Fig. 13, 23) that there are only one or two enveloping ridges to represent the loop. On the other hand, the whorled character of the core can hardly fail to be recognised. The practical difficulties lie almost wholly in rightly classifying a few transitional forms, diagrammatically and roughly expressed in Fig. 11, 4, 5, and Fig. 12, 8, 18, 19, with the words "see" so and so written below, and of which actual examples are given on an enlarged scale in Plates 9 and 10, Figs. 15 and 16. Here Fig. 15, *a* is an undoubted arch, and *c* an undoubted nascent loop; but *b* is transitional between them, though nearer to a loop than an arch. *d* may be thought transitional in the same way, but it has an incipient curl which becomes marked in *e*, while it has grown into a decided whorl in *f*; *d* should also be compared with *j*, which is in some sense a stage towards *k*. *g* is a nascent tented-arch, fully developed in *i*, where the pattern as a whole has a slight slope, but is otherwise fairly symmetrical. In *h* there is some want of symmetry, and a tendency to the formation of a loop on the right side (refer back to Plate 7, Fig. 11, 4, and Fig. 12, 12); it is a transitional case between a tented arch and a loop, with most resemblance to the latter. Plate 10, Fig. 16 illustrates

PLATE 9.

FIG. 15B.

TRANSITIONAL PATTERNS—ARCHES AND LOOPS (enlarged three times).

PLATE 10.

FIG. 16.

TRANSITIONAL PATTERNS—LOOPS AND WHORLS (enlarged three times).

eyed patterns; here *l* and *m* are parts of decided loops; *p*, *q*, and *r* are decided whorls, but *n* is transitional, inclining towards a loop, and *o* is transitional, inclining towards a whorl. *s* is a nascent form of an invaded loop, and is nearly related to *l*; *t* and *u* are decidedly invaded loops.

The Arch–Loop–Whorl, or, more briefly, the A.L.W., system of classification, while in some degree artificial, is very serviceable for preliminary statistics, such as are needed to obtain a broad view of the distribution of the various patterns. A minute subdivision under numerous heads would necessitate a proportional and somewhat overwhelming amount of statistical labour. Fifty-four different standard varieties are by no means an extravagant number, but to treat fifty-four as thoroughly as three would require eighteen times as much material and labour. Effort is economised by obtaining broad results from a discussion of the A.L.W. classes, afterwards verifying or extending them by special inquiries into a few of the further subdivisions.

The divergent ridges that bound any simple pattern admit of nine, and only nine, distinct variations in the first part of their course. The bounding ridge that has attained the summit of any such pattern must have arrived either from the Inner plot (I), the Outer plot (O), or from both. Similarly as regards the bounding ridge that lies at the lowest point of the pattern. Any one of the three former events may occur in connection with any of the three latter events, so they afford in all 3×3, or nine possible combinations. It is convenient to distinguish them by easily intelligible symbols. Thus, let *i* signify a bounding line which starts from the point I, whether it proceeds to the summit or to the base of the pattern; let *o* be a line that similarly proceeds from O, and let *u* be a line that unites the two plots I and O, either by summit or by base. Again, let two symbols be used, of which the first shall always refer to the summit, and the second to the base of the pattern. Then the nine possible cases are—*uu*, *ui*, *uo*; *iu*, *ii*, *io*; *ou*, *oi*, *oo*. The case of the arches is peculiar, but they may be fairly classed under the symbol *uu*.

This easy method of classification has much power. For example, the four possible kinds of simple spirals (see the 1st, 2nd, and the 5th and 6th diagrams in the lowest row of Plate 11, Fig. 17) are wholly determined by the letters *oj*, *jo*, *ij*, *ji*, respectively. The two forms of duplex spirals are similarly determined by *oi* and *io* (see 4th and 5th diagrams in the upper

FIG. 17.

ORIGIN OF SUPPLY OF RIDGES TO PATTERNS OF PRINTS OF RIGHT HAND.

Of the two letters in the left upper corner of each compartment, the first refers to the source of upper boundary of the pattern, the second to the lower boundary.
For patterns on the prints of left hands, *Ii* and *Oo* must be interchanged.

Arches		Rings	Duplex Spirals	
from both sides		from neither side	from both sides	
I and *O* both absent.		*I* and *O* both present	upper supply from	
			I side	*O* side
jj	*jj*	*jj*	*oi*	*io*

Spirals		Loops		Spirals	
from *I* side		from *I* side	from *O* side	from *O* side	
above	below	*I* absent	*O* absent	above	below
oj	*jo*	*oo*	*ii*	*ij*	*ji*

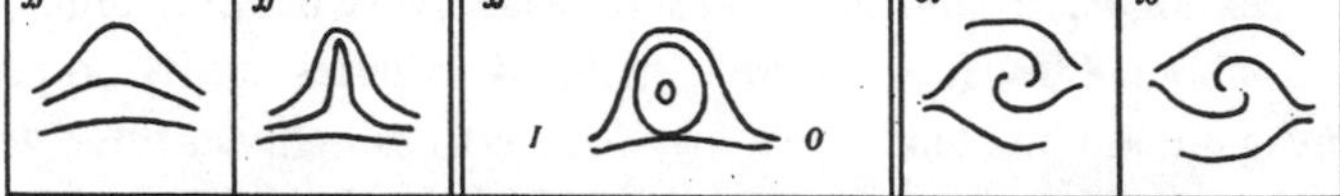

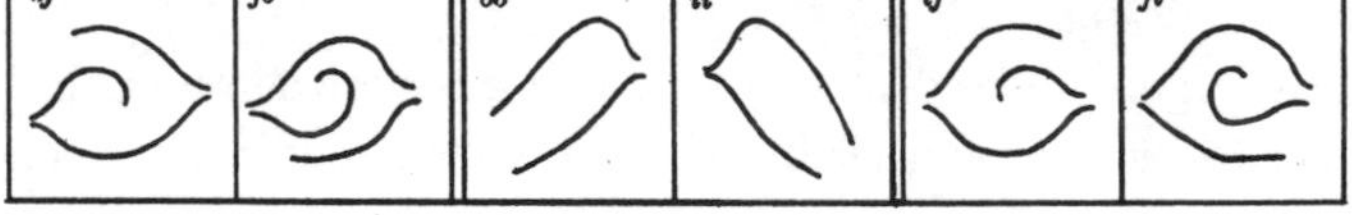

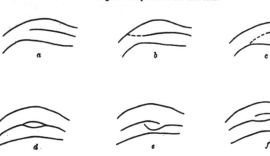

FIG. 18.

Ambiguities in prints of the Minutiæ.

row of Fig. 17), the two slopes of loops by *oo* and *ii* (3rd and 4th in the lower row). It also shows very distinctly the sources whence the streams of ridges proceed that feed the pattern, which itself affords another basis for classification. The resource against uncertainty in respect to ambiguous or difficult patterns is to compile a dictionary of them, with the heads under which it is advisable that they should severally be classed. It would load these pages too heavily to give such a dictionary here. Moreover, it ought to be revised by many experienced eyes, and the time is hardly ripe for this; when it is, it would be no difficult task, out of the large number of prints of separate fingers which for instance I possess (some 15,000), to make an adequate selection, to enlarge them photographically, and finally to print the results in pairs, the one untouched, the other outlined and classified.

It may be asked why ridges are followed and not furrows, the furrow being the real boundary between two systems. The reply is, that the ridges are the easiest to trace; and, as the error through following the ridges cannot exceed one-half of a ridge-interval, I have been content to disregard it. I began by tracing furrows, but preferred the ridges after trial.

Measurements. It has been already shown that when both plots are present (Plate 4, Fig. 8, 4), they form the termini of a base line, from which any part of the pattern may be triangulated, as surveyors would say. Also, that when only one plot exists (3), and the pattern has an axis (which it necessarily has in all ordinary *ii* and *oo* cases), a perpendicular can be let fall upon that axis, whose intersection with it will serve as a second point of reference. But our methods must not be too refined. The centres of the plots are not determinable with real exactness, and repeated prints from so soft a substance as flesh are often somewhat dissimilar, the one being more or less broadened out than the other, owing to unequal pressure. It is therefore well to use such other more convenient points of reference as the particular pattern may present. In loops, the intersection of the axis with the summit of the innermost bend, whether it be a staple or the envelope to a rod (Fig. 14, second and third rows of diagrams), is a well-defined position. In spirals, the centre of the pattern is fairly well defined; also a perpendicular erected from the middle of the base to the outline above and below (Fig. 8, 4) is precise and convenient.

In prints of adults, measurements may be made in absolute units of length, as in fractions of an inch, or else in millimetres. An average ridge-interval makes, however, a better unit, being independent of growth; it is strictly necessary to adopt it in prints made by children, if present measurements are hereafter to be compared with future ones. The simplest plan of determining and employing this unit is to count the number of ridges to the nearest half-ridge, within the space of one-tenth of an inch, measured along the axis of the finger at and about the point where it cuts the *summit* of the outline; then, having already prepared scales suitable for the various likely numbers, to make the measurements with the appropriate scale. Thus, if five ridges were crossed by the axis at that part, in the space of one-tenth of an inch, each unit of the scale to be used would be one-fiftieth of an inch; if there were four ridges, each unit of the scale would be one-fortieth of an inch; if six ridges one-sixtieth, and so forth. There is no theoretical or practical difficulty, only rough indications being required.

It is unnecessary to describe in detail how the bearings of any point may be expressed after the fashion of compass bearings, the direction I–O taking the place of East–West, the uppermost direction that of North, and the lowermost of South. Little more is practically wanted than to be able to describe roughly the position of some remarkable feature in the print, as of an island or an enclosure. A ridge that is characterised by these or any other marked peculiarity is easily identified by the above means, and it thereupon serves as an exact basis for the description of other features.

PURKENJE'S *COMMENTATIO*.

Reference has already been made to Purkenje, who has the honour of being the person who first described the inner scrolls (as distinguished from the outlines of the patterns) formed by the ridges. He did so in a University Thesis delivered at Breslau in 1823, entitled *Commentatio de examine physiologico organi visus et systematis cutanei* (a physiological examination of the visual organ and of the cutaneous system). The thesis is an ill-printed small 8vo pamphlet of fifty-eight pages, written in a form of Latin that is difficult to translate accurately into free English. It is, however, of great historical interest and reputation, having been referred to by nearly all subsequent writers, some of whom there is reason to suspect never saw it, but contented themselves with quoting a very small portion at second-hand. No copy of the pamphlet existed in any public medical library in England, nor in any private one so far as I could learn; neither could I get a sight of it at some important continental libraries. One copy was known of it in America. The very zealous Librarian of the Royal College of Surgeons was so good as to take much pains at my instance, to procure one: his zeal was happily and unexpectedly rewarded by success, and the copy is now securely lodged in the library of the College.

THE TITLE

Commentatio de Examine physiologico organi visus et systematis cutanei quam pro loco in gratioso medicorum ordine rite obtinendo die Dec. 22, 1823. H.X.L.C. publice defendit Johannes Evangelista Purkenje, Med. doctor, Phys. et Path. Professor publicus ordinarius des. Assumto socio Guilielmo Kraus Medicinae studioso.

TRANSLATION, P. 42.

Our attention is next engaged by the wonderful arrangement and curving of the minute furrows connected with the organ of touch[1] on the inner surfaces of the hand and foot, especially on the last phalanx of each finger. Some general account of them is always to be found in every manual of physiology and anatomy, but in an organ of such importance as the human hand, used as it is for very varied movements, and especially serviceable to the sense of touch, no research, however minute, can fail in yielding some gratifying addition to our knowledge of that organ. After numberless observations, I have thus far met with nine principal varieties of curvature according to which the tactile furrows are disposed upon the inner surface of the last phalanx of the fingers. I will describe them concisely, and refer to the diagrams for further explanation (see Plate 12, Fig. 19).

    1. *Transverse flexures.* The minute furrows starting from the bend of the joint, run from one side of the phalanx to the other; at first trans-

---

    1. The Latin is obscure. "Mira vallecularum tangentium in interna parte manus pedisque . . . dispositio flexuraque attentionem . . . in se trahit." There are three ways of translating "tangentium," and none of them makes good sense. In the index of prints he uses the phrase "vallecularum tactui." It would seem that he looked upon the furrows, and not the ridges, as the special seat of touch.

FIG. 19.

THE STANDARD PATTERNS OF PURKENJE.

THE CORES OF THE ABOVE PATTERNS.

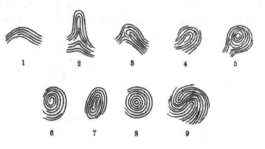

versely in nearly straight lines, then by degrees they become more and more curved towards the middle, until at last they are bent into arches that are almost concentric with the circumference of the finger.

2. *Central Longitudinal Stria.* This configuration is nearly the same as in 1, the only difference being that a perpendicular stria is enclosed within the transverse furrows, as if it were a nucleus.

3. *Oblique Stria.* A solitary line runs from one or other of the two sides of the finger, passing obliquely between the transverse curves in 1, and ending near the middle.

4. *Oblique Sinus.* If this oblique line recurves towards the side from which it started, and is accompanied by several others, all recurved in the same way, the result is an oblique sinus, more or less upright, or horizontal, as the case may be. A junction at its base, of minute lines proceeding from either of its sides, forms a triangle. This distribution of the furrows, in which an oblique sinus is found, is by far the most common, and it may be considered as a special characteristic of man; the furrows that are packed in longitudinal rows are, on the other hand, peculiar to monkeys. The vertex of the oblique sinus is generally inclined towards the radial side of the hand, but it must be observed that the contrary is more frequently the case in the fore-finger, the vertex there tending towards the ulnar side. Scarcely any other configuration is to be found on the toes. The ring finger, too, is often marked with one of the more intricate kinds of pattern, while the remaining fingers have either the oblique sinus or one of the other simpler forms.

5. *Almond.* Here the oblique sinus, as already described, encloses an almond-shaped figure, blunt above, pointed below, and formed of concentric furrows.

6. *Spiral.* When the transverse flexures described in 1 do not pass gradually from straight lines into curves, but assume that form suddenly with a more rapid divergence, a semicircular space is necessarily created, which stands upon the straight and horizontal lines below, as it were upon a base. This space is filled by a spiral either of a simple or composite form. The term 'simple' spiral is to be understood in the usual geometric sense. I call the spiral 'composite' when it is made up of several lines proceeding from the same centre, or of lines branching at intervals and twisted upon themselves. At either side, where the spiral is contiguous to the place at which the straight and curved lines begin to diverge, in order to enclose it, two triangles are formed, just like the single one that is formed at the side of the oblique sinus.

7. *Ellipse,* or *Elliptical Whorl.* The semicircular space described in 6 is here filled with concentric ellipses enclosing a short single line in their middle.

8. *Circle,* or *Circular Whorl.* Here a single point takes the place of the short line mentioned in 7. It is surrounded by a number of concentric circles reaching to the ridges that bound the semicircular space.

9. *Double Whorl.* One portion of the transverse lines runs forward with a bend and recurves upon itself with a half turn, and is embraced by another portion which proceeds from the other side in the same way. This produces a doubly twisted figure which is rarely met with except on the thumb, fore, and ring fingers. The ends of the curved portions may be variously inclined; they may be nearly perpendicular, of various degrees of obliquity, or nearly horizontal.

In all of the forms 6, 7, 8, and 9, triangles may be seen at the points where the divergence begins between the transverse and the arched lines, and at both sides. On the remaining phalanges, the transverse lines proceed diagonally, and are straight or only slightly curved.

(He then proceeds to speak of the palm of the hand in men and in monkeys.)

CHAPTER VI
PERSISTENCE

The evidence that the minutiæ persist throughout life is derived from the scrutiny and comparison of various duplicate impressions, one of each pair having been made many years ago, the other recently. Those which I have studied more or less exhaustively are derived from the digits of fifteen different persons. In some cases repeated impressions of one finger only were available; in most cases of two fingers; in some of an entire hand. Altogether the whole or part of repeated impressions of between twenty and thirty different digits have been studied. I am indebted to Sir W. J. Herschel for almost all these valuable data, without which it would have been impossible to carry on the inquiry. The only other prints are those of Sir W. G——, who, from curiosity, took impressions of his own fingers in sealing-wax in 1874, and fortunately happened to preserve them. He was good enough to make others for me last year, from which photographic prints were made. The following table gives an analysis of the above data. It would be well worth while to hunt up and take the present finger prints of such of the Hindoos as may now be alive, whose impressions were taken in India by Sir W. J. Herschel, and are still preserved. Many years must elapse before my own large collection of finger prints will be available for the purpose of testing persistence during long periods.

The pattern in every distinct finger print, even though it be only a dabbed impression, contains on a rough average thirty-five different points of reference, in addition to its general peculiarities of outline and core. They consist of forkings, beginnings or ends of ridges, islands, and enclosures. These minute details are by no means peculiar to the pattern itself, but are distributed with almost equal abundance throughout the whole palmar surface. In order to make an exhaustive comparison of two impressions they ought to be photographically enlarged to a size not smaller than those shown in Plate 15. Two negatives of impressions can thus be taken side by side on an ordinary quarter-plate, and any number of photographic prints made from them; but, for still more comfortable working, a further enlargement is desirable, say by the prism, p. 55. Some of the prints may be made on ferro-prussiate paper, as already mentioned pp. 55, 56; they are more convenient by far than prints made by the silver or by the platinum process.

Having placed the enlarged prints side by side, two or three conspicuous and convenient points of reference, whether islands, enclosures, or particularly distinct bifurcations, should be identified and marked. By their help, the position of the prints should be readjusted, so that they shall be oriented exactly alike. From each point of reference, in succession, the spines of the ridges are then to be followed with a fine pencil, in the two prints alternately, neatly marking each new point of comparison with a numeral in coloured ink (Plate 13). When both of the prints are good and clear, this is rapidly done; wherever the impressions are faulty, there may be many ambiguities requiring patience to unravel. At first I was timid, and proceeded too hesitatingly when one of the impressions was indistinct, making short alternate traces. Afterwards on gaining confidence, I traced boldly, starting from any well-defined point of reference and not stopping until there were reasonable grounds for hesitation, and found it easy in this way to trace the unions between opposite and incompletely printed ends of ridges, and to disentangle many bad impressions.

An exact correspondence between the *details* of two minutiæ is of secondary importance. Thus, the commonest point of reference is a bifurcation; now the neck or point of divergence of a new ridge is apt to be a little low, and sometimes fails to take the ink; hence a new ridge may appear in one of the prints to have an independent origin, and in the other to be a branch. The *apparent* origin is therefore of little importance, the main fact to be attended to is that a new ridge comes into existence at a particular point; *how* it came into existence is a secondary matter. Simi-

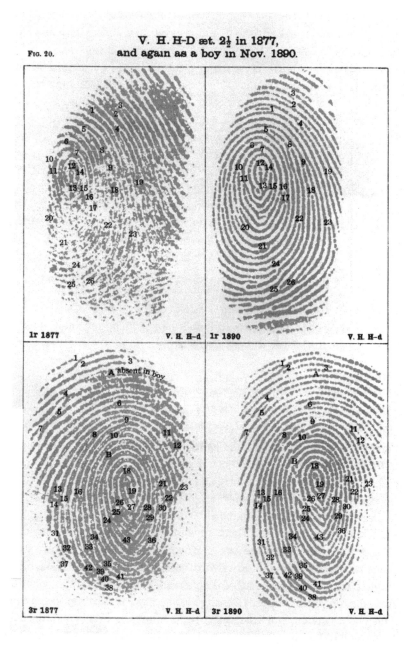

FIG. 20.

**V. H. H-D æt. 2½ in 1877,
and again as a boy in Nov. 1890.**

larly, an apparently broken ridge may in reality be due to an imperfectly printed enclosure; and an island in one print may appear as part of an enclosure in the other. Moreover, this variation in details may be the effect not only of imperfect inking or printing, but of disintegration due to old age, which renders the impressions of the ridges ragged and broken, as in my own finger prints on the title-page.

Plate 11, Fig. 18 explains the nature of the apparent discrepancies better than a verbal description. In *a* a new ridge appears to be suddenly intruded between two adjacent ones, which have separated to make room for it; but a second print, taken from the same finger, may have the appearance of either *b* or *c*, showing that the new ridge is in reality a fork of one or other of them, the low connecting neck having failed to leave an impression. The second line of examples shows how an enclosure which is clearly defined in *d* may give rise to the appearance of broken continuity shown in *e*, and how a distinct island *f* in one of the prints may be the remnant of an enclosure which is shown in the other. These remarks are offered as a caution against attaching undue importance to disaccord in the details of the minutiæ that are found in the same place in different prints. Usually, however, the distinction between a fork and the beginning of a new ridge is clear enough; the islands and enclosures are also mostly well marked.

Plate 13 gives impressions taken from the fingers of a child of 2½ years in 1877, and again in 1890, when a boy of 15. They are enlarged photographically to the same size, and are therefore on different scales. The impressions from the baby-hand are not sharp, but sufficiently distinct for comparison. Every bifurcation, and beginning or ending of a ridge, common to the two impressions, is marked with a numeral in blue ink. There is only one island in the present instance, and that is in the upper pair of prints; it is clearly seen in the right hand print, lying to the left of the inscribed number 13, but the badness of the left hand print makes it hardly decipherable, so it is not numbered. There are a total of twenty-six good points of comparison common to the upper pair of prints; there are forty-three points in the lower pair, forty-two of which appear in both, leaving a single point of disagreement; it is marked A on the fifth ridge counting from the top. Here a bifurcated ridge in the baby is filled up in the boy. This one exception, small though it be, is in my experience unique. The total result of the two pairs of prints is to afford sixty-eight successes and one failure. The student will find it well worth his while to study these and the following prints step by step, to satisfy himself of the extraordinarily exact coincidences between the two members of either of the pairs. Of course the patterns generally must be the same, if the ridges composing them are exactly alike, and the most cursory glance shows them to be so.

Plate 14, Fig. 21 contains rather less than a quarter of each of eight pairs that were published in the *Phil. Trans.* memoir above alluded to. They were there enlarged photographically to twice their natural size, which was hardly enough, as it did not allow sufficient space for inserting the necessary reference numbers. Consequently they have been again considerably enlarged, so much so that it is impossible to put more than a portion of each on the page. However, what is given suffices. The omitted portions may be studied in the memoir. The cases of 1 and 2 are prints of different fingers of the same individual, first as a child 8 years old, and then as a boy of 17. They have been enlarged on the same scale but not to the same size; so the print of the child includes a larger proportion of the original impression than that of the boy. It is therefore only a part of the child's print which is comparable with that of the boy. The remaining six cases refer to four different men, belonging to three quite different families, although their surnames happen to have the same initial, H. They were adults when the first print was made, and from 26 to 31 years older on the second occasion. There is an exact agreement throughout between the two members of each of the eight several couplets.

In the pair 2. A. E. H. Hl., there is an interesting dot at the point 4 (being an island it deserved to have had two numbers, one for the beginning and one for the end). Small as it is, it persists; its growth in size corresponding to the growth of the child in stature.

For the sake of those who are deficient in the colour sense and therefore hardly able, if at all, to distinguish even the blue numerals in Figs. 20, 21, I give an eleventh example, Plate 15, Fig. 22, printed all in black. The numerals are here very legible, but space for their insertion had to be obtained by sacrificing some of the lineations. It is the right fore-finger of Sir W. Herschel and has been already published twice; first in the account of my lecture at the Royal Institution, and secondly, in its present conspicuous form, in my paper in the *Nineteenth Century*. The number of years that elapsed between the two impressions is thirty-one, and the prints con-

FIG. 21.

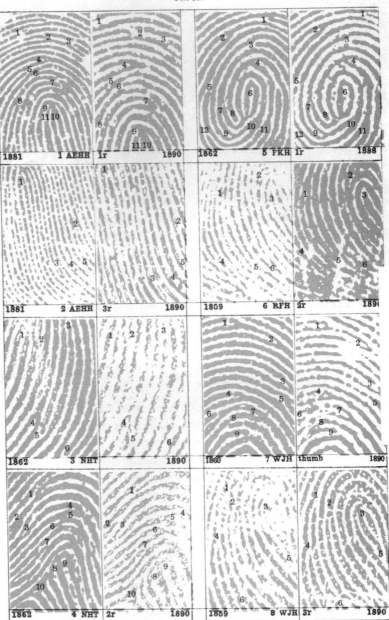

tain twenty-four points of comparison, all of which will be seen to agree. I also possess a later print than this, taken in 1890 from the same finger, which tells the same tale.

The final result of the prints in these pages is that they give photographic enlargements of the whole or portions of eleven couplets belonging to six different persons, who are members of five unrelated families, and which contain between them 158 points of comparison, of which only one failed. Adding the portions of the prints that are omitted here, but which will be found in the *Phil. Trans.*, the material that I have thus far published contains 389 points of comparison, of which one failed. The details are given in the annexed table—

Order in the Figs.	Initials.	Digit of right hand.	Age at date of first print.	Dates of the two prints. 1st. 2nd.	Years elapsed between the two prints	Total points of agreement in	
						Figs. 20 and 21	Figs. 20, 22, and in *Ph. Trans.*
FIG. 20							
1.	V. H. Hd.	Fore	2½	1877–90	13	26	26
2.	V. H. Hd.	Ring	2½	1877–90	13	42	42
FIG. 21							
1.	A. E. H. Hl.	Fore	8	1881–90	9	11	33
2.	A. E. H. Hl.	Ring	8	1881–90	9	5	36
3.	N. H. Tn.	Fore	28	1862–90	28	6	27
4.	N. H. Tu.	Middle	28	1862–90	28	10	36
5.	F. K. Ht.	Fore	28	1862–88	26	12	55
6.	R. F. Hn.	Middle	31	1859–90	31	6	27
7.	W. J. Hl.	Thumb	30	1860–90	30	9	50
8.	W. J. Hl.	Ring	31	1859–90	31	6	32
FIG. 22							
1.	W. J. Hl.	Fore	31	1859–90	31	24	24
			Total points of agreement			157	388
			Do. of disagreement . . .			71	1

Fig. 22.

RIGHT FOREFINGER of Sir W. J. H. in 1860 and in 1888.

in 1860　　　　　　　　*in 1888*

Fig. 23.

DISTRIBUTION of the PERIODS of LIFE, to which the evidence of persistency refers.

Persons.	Age at first print.	Interval in years.	Age at second print.	Ages, 0—80 years.						
				10	20	30	40	50	60	70
H. H—d	2	13	15							
A. H—l	4	12	16							
J. H—l	8	13	21							
E. H—l	10	13	23							
W. J. H—l	26	30	56							
R. F. H—n	26	31	57							
N. H. T—n	27	28	55							
F. H. H—t	27	26	53							
W. G—e	62	17	79							

It is difficult to give a just estimate of the number of points of comparison that I have studied in other couplets of prints, because they were not examined as exhaustively as in these. There were no less than one hundred and eleven of them in the ball of the thumb of the child V. H. Hd., besides twenty-five in the imperfect prints of his middle and little fingers; these alone raise the total of 389 to 525. I must on the whole have looked for more than 700 points of comparison, and have found agreement in every single case that was examined, except the one already mentioned in Fig. 20, of a ridge that was split in the child, but had closed up some few years later.

The prints in the two plates cover the intervals from childhood to boyhood, from boyhood to early manhood, from manhood to about the age of 60, and another set—that of Sir W. G.—covers the interval from 67 to 80. This is clearly expressed by the diagram (Plate 15, Fig. 23). As there is no sign, except in one case, of change during any one of these four intervals, which together almost wholly cover the ordinary life of man, we are justified in inferring that between birth and death there is absolutely no change in, say, 699 out of 700 of the numerous characteristics in the markings of the fingers of the same person, such as can be impressed by them whenever it is desirable to do so. Neither can there be any change after death, up to the time when the skin perishes through decomposition; for example, the marks on the fingers of many Egyptian mummies, and on the paws of stuffed monkeys, still remain legible. Very good evidence and careful inquiry is thus seen to justify the popular idea of the persistence of finger markings, that has hitherto been too rashly jumped at, and which wrongly ascribed the persistence to the general appearance of the pattern, rather than to the minutiæ it contains. There appear to be no external bodily characteristics, other than deep scars and tattoo marks, comparable in their persistence to these markings, whether they be on the finger, on other parts of the palmar surface of the hand, or on the sole of the foot. At the same time they are out of all proportion more numerous than any other measurable features; about thirty-five of them are situated on the bulb of each of the ten digits, in addition to more than 100 on the ball of the thumb, which has not one-fifth of the superficies of the rest of the palmar surface. The total number of points suitable for comparison on the two hands must therefore be not less than one thousand and nearer to two; an estimate which I verified by a rough count on my own hand; similarly in respect to the feet. The dimensions of the limbs and body alter in the course of growth and decay; the colour, quantity, and quality of the hair, the tint and quality of the skin, the number and set of the teeth, the expression of the features, the gestures, the handwriting, even the eye-colour, change after many years. There seems no persistence in the visible parts of the body, except in these minute and hitherto too much disregarded ridges.

It must be emphasised that it is in the minutiæ, and *not* in the measured dimensions of any portion of the pattern, that this remarkable persistence is observed, not even if the measurements be made in units of a ridge-interval. The pattern grows simultaneously with the finger, and its proportions vary with its fatness, leanness, usage, gouty deformation, or age. But, though the pattern as a whole may become considerably altered in length or breadth, the number of ridges, their embranchments, and other minutiæ remain unchanged. So it is with the pattern on a piece of lace. The piece as a whole may be stretched in this way, or shrunk in that, and its outline altogether altered; nevertheless every one of the component threads, and every knot in every thread, can easily be traced and identified in both. Therefore, in speaking of the persistence of the marks on the finger, the phrase must be taken to apply principally to the minutiæ, and to the general character of the pattern; not to the measure of its length, breadth, or other diameter; these being no more constant than the stature, or any other of the ordinary anthropometric data.

CHAPTER VII
EVIDENTIAL VALUE

The object of this chapter is to give an approximate numerical idea of the value of finger prints as a means of Personal Identification. Though the estimates that will be made are professedly and obviouly far below the truth, they are amply sufficient to prove that the evidence afforded by finger prints may be trusted in a most remarkable degree.

Our problem is this: given two finger prints, which are alike in their minutiæ, what is the chance that they were made by different persons?

The first attempt at comparing two finger prints would be directed to a rough general examination of their respective patterns. If they do not agree in being arches, loops, or whorls, there can be no doubt that the prints are those of different fingers, neither can there be doubt when they are distinct forms of the same general class. But to agree thus far goes only a short way towards establishing identity, for the number of patterns that are promptly distinguishable from one another is not large. My earlier inquiries showed this, when endeavouring to sort the prints of 1000 thumbs into groups that differed each from the rest by an "equally discernible" interval. While the attempt, as already mentioned, was not successful in its main object, it showed that nearly all the collection could be sorted into 100 groups, in each of which the prints had a fairly near resemblance. Moreover, twelve or fifteen of the groups referred to different varieties of the loop; and as two-thirds of all the prints are loops, two-thirds of the 1000 specimens fell into twelve or fifteen groups. The

chance that an unseen pattern is some particular variety of loop, is therefore compounded of 2 to 3 against its being a loop at all, and of 1 to 12
or 15, as the case may be, against its being the specified kind of loop. This
makes an adverse chance of only 2 to 36, or to 45, say, as 2 to 40, or as 1
to 20. This very rude calculation suffices to show that on the average, no
great reliance can be placed on a general resemblance in the appearance
of two finger prints, as a proof that they were made by the same finger,
though the obvious disagreement of two prints is conclusive evidence that
they were made by different fingers.

When we proceed to a much more careful comparison, and collate
successively the numerous minutiæ, their coincidence throughout would
be an evidence of identity, whose value we will now try to appraise.

Let us first consider the question, how far may the minutiæ, or groups
of them, be treated as *independent* variables?

Suppose that a tiny square of paper of only one average ridge-interval
in the side, be cut out and dropped at random on a finger print; it will
mask from view a minute portion of one, or possibly of two ridges. There
can be little doubt that what was hidden could be correctly interpolated
by simply joining the ends of the ridge or ridges that were interrupted. It
is true, the paper might possibly have fallen exactly upon, and hidden, a
minute island or enclosure, and that our reconstruction would have failed
in consequence, but such an accident is improbable in a high degree, and
maybe almost ignored.

Repeating the process with a much larger square of paper, say, of
twelve ridge-intervals in the side, the improbability of correctly recon-
structing the masked portion will have immensely increased. The number
of ridges that enter the square on any one side will perhaps, as often as
not, differ from the number which emerge from the opposite side; and
when they are the same, it does not at all follow that they would be continuous each to each, for in so large a space forks and junctions are sure
to occur between some, and it is impossible to know which, of the ridges.
Consequently, there must exist a certain size of square with more than one
and less than twelve ridge-intervals in the side, which will mask so much
of the print, that it will be an even chance whether the hidden portion can,
on the average, be rightly reconstructed or not. The size of that square
must now be considered.

If the reader will refer to Plate 14, in which there are eight much enlarged photographs of portions of different finger prints, he will observe that the length of each of the portions exceeds the breadth in the proportion of 3 to 2. Consequently, by drawing one line down the middle and two lines across, each portion may be divided into six squares. Moreover, it will be noticed that the side of each of these squares has a length of about six ridge-intervals. I cut out squares of paper of this size, and throwing one of them at random on any one of the eight portions, succeeded almost as frequently as not in drawing lines on its back which comparison afterwards showed to have followed the true course of the ridges. The provisional estimate that a length of six ridge-intervals approximated to but exceeded that of the side of the desired square, proved to be correct by the following more exact observations, and by three different methods.

I. The first set of tests to verify this estimate were made upon photographic enlargements of various thumb prints, to double their natural size. A six-ridge-interval square of paper was damped and laid at random on the print, the core of the pattern, which was too complex in many cases to serve as an average test, being alone avoided. The prints being on ordinary albuminised paper, which is slightly adherent when moistened, the patch stuck temporarily wherever it was placed and pressed down. Next, a sheet of tracing-paper, which we will call No. 1, was laid over all, and the margin of the square patch was traced upon it, together with the course of the surrounding ridges up to that margin. Then I interpolated on the tracing-paper what seemed to be the most likely course of those ridges which were hidden by the square. No. 1 was then removed, and a second sheet, No. 2, was laid on, and the margin of the patch was outlined on it as before, together with the ridges leading up to it. Next, a corner only of No. 2 was raised, the square patch was whisked away from underneath, the corner was replaced, the sheet was flattened down, and the actual courses of the ridges within the already marked outline were traced in. Thus there were two tracings of the margin of the square, of which No. 1 contained the ridges as I had interpolated them, No. 2 as they really were, and it was easy to compare the two. The results are given in the first column of the following table—

INTERPOLATION OF RIDGES IN A SIX-RIDGE-INTERVAL SQUARE.

Result.	Double Enlargements.	Six-fold scales with prism.	Twenty-fold scale with chequer-work.	Total.
Right	12	8	7	27
Wrong	20	12	16	48
Total	32	20	23	75

II. In the second method the tracing-papers were discarded, and the prism of a camera lucida used. It threw an image three times the size of the photo-enlargement, upon a card, and there it was traced. The same general principle was adopted as in the first method, but the results being on a larger scale, and drawn on stout paper, were more satisfactory and convenient. They are given in the second column of the table. In this and the foregoing methods two different portions of the same print were sometimes dealt with, for it was a little more convenient and seemed as good a way of obtaining average results as that of always using portions of different finger prints. The total number of fifty-two trials; by one or other of the two methods, were made from about forty different prints. (I am not sure of the exact number.)

The results in each of the two methods were sometimes quite right, sometimes quite wrong, sometimes neither one nor the other. The latter depended on the individual judgment as to which class it belonged, and might be battled over with more or less show of reason by advocates on opposite sides. Equally dividing these intermediate cases between "right" and "wrong," the results were obtained as shown. In one, and only one, of the cases, the most reasonable interpretation had not been given, and the result had been wrong when it ought to have been right. The purely personal error was therefore disregarded, and the result entered as "right."

III. A third attempt was made by a different method, upon the lineations of a finger print drawn on about a twenty-fold scale. It had first been enlarged four times by photography, and from this enlargement the axes of the ridges had been drawn with a five-fold enlarging pantagraph. The aim now was to reconstruct the entire finger print by two successive and independent acts of interpolation. A sheet of transparent tracing-paper was ruled into six-ridge-interval squares, and every one of its alternate squares was rendered opaque by pasting white paper upon it, giving it the appearance of a chess-board. When this chequer-work was laid on the print, exactly one half of the six-ridge squares were masked by the opaque squares, while the ridges running up to them could be seen. They were not quite so visible as if each opaque square had been wholly detached from its neighbours, instead of touching them at the extreme corners, still the loss of information thereby occasioned was small, and not worth laying stress upon. It is easily understood that when the chequer-work was moved parallel to itself, through the space of one square, whether upwards or downwards, or to the right or left, the parts that were previously masked became visible, and those that were visible became masked. The object was to interpolate the ridges in every opaque square under one of these conditions, then to do the same for the remaining squares under the other condition, and finally, by combining the results, to obtain a complete scheme of the ridges wholly by interpolation. This was easily done by using two sheets of tracing-paper, laid in succession over the chequer-work, whose position on the print had been changed meanwhile, and afterwards tracing the lineations that were drawn on one of the two sheets upon the vacant squares of the other. The results are given in the third column of the table.

The three methods give roughly similar results, and we may therefore accept the ratios of their totals, which is 27 to 75, or say 1 to 3, as representing the chance that the reconstruction of any six-ridge-interval square would be correct under the given conditions. On reckoning the chance as 1 to 2, which will be done at first, it is obvious that the error, whatever it may be, is on the safe side. A closer equality in the chance that the ridges in a square might run in the observed way or in some other way, would result from taking a square of five ridge-intervals in the side. I believe this to be very closely the right size. A four-ridge-interval square is certainly too small.

When the reconstructed squares were wrong, they had none the less a natural appearance. This was especially seen, and on a large scale, in the result of the method by chequer-work, in which the lineations of an entire print were constructed by guess. Being so familiar with the run of these ridges in finger prints, I can speak with confidence on this. My assumption is, that any one of these reconstructions represents lineations that might have occurred in Nature, in association with the conditions outside the square, just as well as the lineations of the actual finger print. The courses of the ridges in each square are subject to uncertainties, due to petty *local* incidents, to which the conditions outside the square give no sure indication. They appear to be in great part determined by the particular disposition of each one or more of the half hundred or so sweat-glands which the square contains. The ridges rarely run in evenly flowing lines, but may be compared to footways across a broken country, which, while they follow a general direction, are continually deflected by such trifles as a tuft of grass, a stone, or a puddle. Even if the number of ridges emerging from a six-ridge-interval square equals the number of those which enter, it does not follow that they run across in parallel lines, for there is plenty of room for any one of the ridges to end, and another to bifurcate. It is impossible, therefore, to know beforehand in which, if in any of the ridges, these peculiarities will be found. When the number of entering and issuing ridges is unequal, the difficulty is increased. There may, moreover, be islands or enclosures in any particular part of the square. It therefore seems right to look upon the squares as independent variables, in the sense that when the surrounding conditions are alone taken into account, the ridges within their limits may either run in the observed way or in a different way, the chance of these two contrasted events being taken (for safety's sake) as approximately equal.

In comparing finger prints which are alike in their general pattern, it may well happen that the proportions of the patterns differ; one may be that of a slender boy, the other that of a man whose fingers have been broadened or deformed by ill usage. It is therefore requisite to imagine that only one of the prints is divided into exact squares, and to suppose that a reticulation has been drawn over the other, in which each mesh included the corresponding parts of the former print. Frequent trials have shown that there is no practical difficulty in actually doing this, and it is the only way of making a fair comparison between the two.

These six-ridge-interval squares may thus be regarded as independent units, each of which is equally liable to fall into one or other of two alternative classes, when the surrounding conditions are alone known. The inevitable consequence from this datum is that the chance of an exact correspondence between two different finger prints, in each of the six-ridge-interval squares into which they may be divided, and which are about 24 in number, is at least as 1 to 2 multiplied into itself 24 times (usually written 2^{24}), that is as 1 to about ten thousand millions. But we must not forget that the six-ridge square was taken in order to ensure under-estimation, a five-ridge square would have been preferable, so the adverse chances would in reality be enormously greater still.

It is hateful to blunder in calculations of adverse chances, by over-looking correlations between variables, and to falsely assume them independent, with the result that inflated estimates are made which require to be proportionately reduced. Here, however, there seems to be little room for such an error.

We must next combine the above enormously unfavourable chance, which we will call a, with the other chances of not guessing correctly beforehand the surrounding conditions under which a was calculated. These latter are divisible into b and c; the chance b is that of not guessing correctly the general course of the ridges adjacent to each square, and c that of not guessing rightly the number of ridges that enter and issue from the square. The chance b has already been discussed, with the result that it might be taken as 1 to 20 for two-thirds of all the patterns. It would be higher for the remainder, and very high indeed for some few of them, but as it is advisable always to underestimate, it may be taken as 1 to 20; or, to obtain the convenience of dealing only with values of 2 multiplied into itself, the still lower ratio of 1 to 2^4, that is as 1 to 16. As to the remaining chance c with which a and b have to be compounded, namely, that of guessing aright the number of ridges that enter and leave each side of a particular square, I can offer no careful observations. The number of the ridges would for the most part vary between five and seven, and those in the different squares are certainly not quite independent of one another. We have already arrived at such large figures that it is surplusage to heap up more of them, therefore, let us say, as a mere nominal sum much below the real figure, that the chance against guessing each and every one of these data correctly is as 1 to 250, or say 1 to 2^8 (= 256).

The result is, that the chance of lineations, constructed by the imagination according to strictly natural forms, which shall be found to resemble those of a single finger print in all their minutiæ, is less than 1 to $2^{24} \times 2^4 \times 2^8$, or 1 to 2^{36}, or 1 to about sixty-four thousand millions. The inference is, that as the number of the human race is reckoned at about sixteen thousand millions, it is a smaller chance than 1 to 4 that the print of a *single* finger of any given person would be exactly like that of the same finger of any other member of the human race.

When two fingers of each of the two persons are compared, and found to have the same minutiæ, the improbability of 1 to 2^{36} becomes squared and reaches a figure altogether beyond the range of the imagination; when three fingers, it is cubed, and so on.

A single instance has shown that the minutiæ are *not* invariably permanent throughout life, but that one or more of them may possibly change. They may also be destroyed by wounds, and more or less disintegrated by hard work, disease, or age. Ambiguities will thus arise in their interpretation, one person asserting a resemblance in respect to a particular feature, while another asserts dissimilarity. It is therefore of interest to know how far a conceded resemblance in the great majority of the minutiæ combined with some doubt as to the remainder, will tell in favour of identity. It will now be convenient to change our datum from a six-ridge to a five-ridge square of which about thirty-five are contained in a single print, 35×5^2 or 35×25 being much the same as 24×6^2 or 24×36. The reason for the change is that this number of thirty-five happens to be the same as that of the minutiæ. We shall therefore not be acting unfairly if, with reservation, and for the sake of obtaining some result, however rough, we consider the thirty-five minutiæ themselves as so many independent variables, and accept the chance now as 1 to 2^{35}.

This has to be multiplied, as before, into the factor of $2^4 \times 2^8$ (which may still be considered appropriate, though it is too small), making the total of adverse chances 1 to 2^{35}.Upon such a basis, the calculation is simple. There would on the average be 47 instances, out of the total 2^{47} combinations, of similarity in all but one particular; $^{47 \times 46}/_{1 \times 2}$ in all but two; $^{47 \times 46 \times 45}/_{1 \times 2 \times 3}$ in all but three, and so on according to the well-known binomial expansion. Taking for convenience the powers of 2 to which these values approximate, or rather with the view of not overestimating, let us take the power of 2 that falls short of each of them; these may be reckoned as respectively equal to 2^6, 2^{10}, 2^{14}, 2^{18}, etc. Hence the roughly approximate chances of resemblance in all particulars are as 2^{47} to 1; in all particulars but one, as 2^{47-6}, or 2^{41} to 1; in all but two, as 2^{37} to 1; in all but three, as 2^{33} to 1; in all but four, as 2^{29} to 1. Even 2^{29} is so large as to require a row of nine figures to express it. Hence a few instances of dissimilarity in the two prints of a single finger, still leave untouched an enormously large residue of evidence in favour of identity, and when two, three, or more fingers in the two persons agree to that extent, the strength of the evidence rises by squares, cubes, etc., far above the level of that amount of probability which begins to rank as certainty.

Whatever reductions a legitimate criticism may make in the numerical results arrived at in this chapter, bearing in mind the occasional ambiguities pictured in Fig. 18, the broad fact remains, that a complete or nearly complete accordance between two prints of a single finger, and vastly more so between the prints of two or more fingers, affords evidence requiring no corroboration, that the persons from whom they were made are the same. Let it also be remembered, that this evidence is applicable not only to adults, but can establish the identity of the same person at any stage of his life between babyhood and old age, and for some time after his death.

We read of the dead body of Jezebel being devoured by the dogs of Jezreel, so that no man might say, "This is Jezebel," and that the dogs left only her skull, the palms of her hands, and the soles of her feet; but the palms of the hands and the soles of the feet are the very remains by which a corpse might be most surely identified, if impressions of them, made during life, were available.

Chapter VIII

Peculiarities of the Digits

The data used in this chapter are the prints of 5000 different digits, namely, the ten digits of 500 different persons; each digit can thus be treated, both separately and in combination, in 500 cases. Five hundred cannot be called a large number, but it suffices for approximate results; the percentages that it yields may, for instance, be expected to be trustworthy, more often than not, within two units.

When preparing the tables for this chapter, I gave a more liberal interpretation to the word "Arch" than subsequently. At first, every pattern between a Forked-Arch and a Nascent-Loop (Plate 7) was rated as an Arch; afterwards they were rated as Loops.

The relative frequency of the three several classes in the 5000 digits was as follows—

Arches ......6.5 per cent.
Loops ......67.5 per cent.
Whorls .....26.0 per cent.
Total ......100.0 per cent.

From this it appears, that on the average out of every 15 or 16 digits, one has an arch; out of every 3 digits, two have loops; out of every 4 digits, one has a whorl.

This coarse statistical treatment leaves an inadequate impression, each digit and each hand having its own peculiarity, as we shall see in the following table—

TABLE I.

Percentage frequency of Arches, Loops, and Whorls on the different digits, from observations of the 5000 digits of 500 persons.

Digit.	RIGHT HAND.				LEFT HAND.			
	Arch.	Loop.	Whorl.	Total	Arch.	Loop.	Whorl.	Total.
Thumb	3	53	44	100	5	65	30	100
Fore-finger	17	53	30	100	17	55	16	100
Middle do.	7	78	15	100	8	76	16	100
Ring do.	2	53	45	100	3	66	31	100
Little do.	1	86	13	100	2	90	8	100
Total	30	323	147	500	35	352	113	500

The percentage of arches on the various digits varies from 1 to 17; of loops, from 53 to 90; of whorls, from 13 to 45, consequently the statistics of the digits must be separated, and not massed indiscriminately.

Are the A.L.W. patterns distributed in the same way upon the corresponding digits of the two hands? The answer from the last table is distinct and curious, and will be best appreciated on re-arranging the entries as follows—

TABLE II.

Digit.	ARCHES.		LOOPS.		WHORLS.	
	Right.	Left.	Right.	Left.	Right.	Left.
Fore-Finger	17	17	53	53	30	28
Middle do.	7	8	78	76	15	16
Little do.	1	2	86	90	13	8
Thumb.	3	5	53	65	44	30
Ring do.	2	3	53	66	45	31
Total 1000	30	35	323	350	147	113

The digits are seen to fall into two well-marked groups; the one including the fore, middle, and little fingers, the other including the thumb and ringfinger. As regards the first group, the frequency with which any pattern occurs in any named digit is statistically the same, whether that digit be on the right or on the left hand; as regards the second group, the frequency differs greatly in the two hands. But though in the first group the two fore-fingers, the two middle, and the two little fingers of the right hand are severally circumstanced alike in the frequency with which their various patterns occur, the difference between the frequency of the patterns on a fore, a middle, and a little finger, respectively, is very great.

In the second group, though the thumbs on opposite hands do not resemble each other in the statistical frequency of the A.L.W. patterns, nor do the ring-fingers, there is a great resemblance between the respective frequencies in the thumbs and ring-fingers; for instance, the Whorls on either of these fingers on the left hand are only two-thirds as common as those on the right. The figures in each line and in each column are consistent throughout in expressing these curious differences, which must therefore be accepted as facts, and not as statistical accidents, whatever may be their explanation.

One of the most noticeable peculiarities in Table I. is the much greater frequency of Arches on the fore-fingers than on any other of the four digits. It amounts to 17 per cent on the fore-fingers, while on the thumbs and on the remaining fingers the frequency diminishes (Table III.) in a ratio that roughly accords with the distance of each digit from the fore-finger.

TABLE III.

Percentage frequency of Arches.					
Hand.	Thumb.	Fore-finger.	Middle finger.	Ring-finger.	Little finger.
Right ...	3	17	7	2	1
Left.	5	17	8	3	4
Mean ...	4	17	7.5	2.5	2.5

The frequency of Loops (Table IV.) has two maxima; the principal one is on the little finger, the secondary on the middle finger.

TABLE IV.

Percentage frequency of Loops.					
Hand.	Thumb.	Fore-finger.	Middle finger.	Ring-finger.	Little finger.
Right ...	53	53	78	66	86
Left.....	65	55	76	53	90
Mean ...	59	54	77	59.5	88

Whorls (Table V.) are most common on the thumb and the ring-finger, most rare on the middle and little fingers.

TABLE V.

Percentage frequency of Whorls.					
Hand.	Thumb.	Fore-finger.	Middle finger.	Ring-finger.	Little finger.
Right ...	44	30	15	45	13
Left.....	30	28	16	31	8
Mean ...	37	29	15.5	38	10.5

The fore-finger is peculiar in the frequency with which the direction of the slopes of its loops differs from that which is by far the most common in all other digits. A loop *must* have a slope, being caused by the disposition of the ridges into the form of a pocket, opening downwards to one or other side of the finger. If it opens towards the inner or thumb side of the hand, it will be called an inner slope; if towards the outer or little-finger side, it will be called an outer slope. In all digits, except the fore-fingers, the inner slope is much the more rare of the two; but in the fore-fingers the inner slope appears two-thirds as frequently as the outer slope. Out of the percentage of 53 loops of the one or other kind on the right fore-finger, 21 of them have an inner and 32 an outer slope; out of the percentage of 55 loops on the left fore-finger, 21 have inner and 34 have outer slopes. These subdivisions 21–21 and 32–34 corroborate the strong statistical similarity that was observed to exist between the frequency of the several patterns on the right and left fore-fingers; a condition which was also found to characterise the middle and little fingers.

It is strange that Purkenje considers the "inner" slope on the fore-finger to be more frequent than the "outer" (p. 89, 4). My nomenclature differs from his, but there is no doubt as to the disagreement in meaning. The facts to be adduced hereafter make it most improbable that the persons observed were racially unlike in this particular.

The tendencies of digits to resemble one another will now be considered in their various combinations. They will be taken two at a time, in order to learn the frequency with which both members of the various couplets are affected by the same A.L.W. class of pattern. Every combination will be discussed, except those into which the little finger enters. These are omitted, because the overwhelming frequency of loops in the little fingers would make the results of comparatively little interest, while their insertion would greatly increase the size of the table.

TABLE VIa.

Percentage of cases in which the same class of pattern occurs in the same digits of the two hands. (From observation of 5000 digits of 500 persons.)				
Couplets of Digits.	Arches.	Loops.	Whorls.	Total.
The two thumbs	2	48	24	74
" fore-fingers . . .	9	38	20	67
" middle fingers .	3	65	9	77
" ring-fingers	2	46	26	74
Mean of the Totals 72				

TABLE VIb.

Percentage of cases in which the same class of pattern occurs in various couplets of different digits. (From 500 persons as above.)								
Couplets of Digits.	Of Same Hands.				Of Opposite Hands.			
	Arch.	Loops.	Whorls.	Total.	Arch.	Loops.	Whorls.	Total.
Thumb and fore-finger	2	35	16	53	2	33	15	50
Thumb and middle finger	1	48	9	58	1	47	8	56
Thumb and ring-finger	1	40	20	61	1	38	18	57
Fore and middle finger	5	48	12	65	5	46	11	62
Fore and ring-finger	2	35	17	54	2	35	17	54
Middle and ring-finger	2	50	13	65	2	50	12	64
Means of the Totals.............59					57			

A striking feature in this last table is the close similarity between corresponding entries relating to the same and to the opposite hands. There are eighteen sets to be compared; namely, six couplets of different names, in each of which the frequency of three different classes of patterns is discussed. The eighteen pairs of corresponding couplets are closely alike in every instance. It is worth while to rearrange the figures as below, for the greater convenience of observing their resemblances.

TABLE VII.

Couplet.	Arches in		Loops in		Whorls in	
	Same hand.	Opposite hand.	Same hand.	Opposite hand.	Same hand	Opposite hand
Thumb and fore-finger	2	2	35	33	16	15
Thumb and middle finger	1	1	48	47	9	8
Thumb and ring-finger	1	1	40	38	20	18
Fore and middle finger	5	5	48	46	12	11
Fore and ring-finger	2	2	35	35	17	17
Middle and ring-finger	2	2	50	50	13	12

The agreement in the above entries is so curiously close as to have excited grave suspicion that it was due to some absurd blunder, by which the same figures were made inadvertently to do duty twice over, but subsequent checking disclosed no error. Though the unanimity of the results is wonderful, they are fairly arrived at, and leave no doubt that the relationship of any one particular digit, whether thumb, fore, middle, ring or little finger, to any other particular digit, is the same, whether the two digits are on the same or on opposite hands. It would be a most interesting subject of statistical inquiry to ascertain whether the distribution of malformations, or of the various forms of skin disease among the digits, corroborates this unexpected and remarkable result. I am sorry to have no means of undertaking it, being assured on good authority that no adequate collection of the necessary data has yet been published.

It might be hastily inferred from the statistical identity of the connection between, say, the right thumb and each of the two fore-fingers, that the patterns on the two fore-fingers ought always to be alike, whether arch, loop, or whorl. If X, it may be said, is identical both with Y and with Z, then Y and Z must be identical with one another. But the statement of the problem is wrong; X is not identical with Y and Z, but only bears an identical amount of statistical resemblance to each of them; so this reasoning is inadmissible. The character of the pattern on any digit is determined by causes of whose precise nature we are ignorant; but we may rest assured that they are numerous and variable, and that their variations are in large part independent of one another. We can in imagination divide them into groups, calling those that are common to the thumb and the fore-finger of either hand, and to those couplets exclusively, the A causes; those that are common to the two thumbs and to these exclusively, the B causes; and similarly those common to the two fore-fingers exclusively, the C causes.

Then the sum of the variable causes determining the class of pattern in the four several digits now in question are these—

Right thumb	$A + B +$ an unclassed residue called $X_{(1)}$
Left thumb	$A + B +$ „ „ „ $X_{(2)}$
Right fore-finger	$A + C +$ „ „ „ $Z_{(1)}$
Left fore-finger	$A + C +$ „ „ „ $Z_{(2)}$

The nearness of relationship between the two thumbs is sufficiently indicated by a fraction that expresses the proportion between all the causes common to the two thumbs exclusively, and the totality of the causes by which the A.L.W. class of the patterns of the thumbs is determined, that is to say, by

$$\frac{A + B}{A + B + X_{(1)} + X_{(2)}} \quad \dots\dots\dots\dots\dots\dots (1)$$

Similarly, the nearness of the relationship between the two fore-fingers by

$$\frac{A + C}{A + C + Z_{(1)} + Z_{(2)}} \quad \dots\dots\dots\dots\dots\dots (2)$$

And that between a thumb and a fore-finger by

$$\frac{A}{A + B + C + X_{(1)} \text{ (or } X_{(2)}) + Z_{(1)} \text{ (or } Z_{(2)})} \quad \dots\dots\dots\dots (3)$$

The fractions (1) and (2) being both greater than (3), it follows that the relationships between the two thumbs, or between the two fore-fingers, are closer than that between the thumb and either fore-finger; at the same time it is clear that neither of the two former relationships is so close as to reach identity. Similarly as regards the other couplets of digits. The tabular entries fully confirm this deduction, for, without going now into further details, it will be seen from the "Mean of the Totals" at the bottom line of Table VI*b* that the average percentage of cases in which two different digits have the same class of patterns, whether they be on the same or on opposite hands, is 59 or 57 (say 58), while the average percentage of cases in which right and left digits bearing the same name have the same class of pattern (Table VI*a*) is 72. This is barely two-thirds of the 100 which would imply identity. At the same time, the 72 considerably exceeds the 58.

Let us now endeavour to measure the relationships between the various couplets of digits on a well-defined centesimal scale, first recalling the fundamental principles of the connection that subsists between relationships of all kinds, whether between digits, or between kinsmen, or between any of those numerous varieties of related events with which statisticians deal.

Relationships are all due to the joint action of two groups of variable causes, the one common to both of the related objects, the other special to each, as in the case just discussed. Using an analogous nomenclature to that already employed, the peculiarity of one of the two objects is due to an aggregate of variable causes that we may call C + X, and that of the other to C + Z, in which C are the causes common to both, and X and Z the special ones. In exact proportion as X and Z diminish, and C becomes of overpowering effect, so does the closeness of the relationship increase. When X and Z both disappear, the result is identity of character. On the other hand, when C disappears, all relationship ceases, and the variations of the two objects are strictly independent. The simplest case is that in which X and Z are equal, and *in this*, it becomes easy to devise a scale in which 0° shall stand for no relationship, and 100° for identity, and upon which the intermediate degrees of relationship may be marked at their proper value. Upon this assumption, but with some misgiving, I will attempt to subject the digits to this form of measurement. It will save time first to work out an example, and then, after gaining in that way, a clearer understanding of what the process is, to discuss its defects. Let us select for our example the case that brings out these defects in the most conspicuous manner, as follows—

Table V. tells us that the percentage of whorls in the right ring-finger is 45, and in the left ring-finger 31. Table VI*a* tells us that the percentage of the double event of a whorl occurring on both the ring-fingers of the same person is 26. It is required to express the relationship between the right and left ring-fingers on a centesimal scale, in which 0° shall stand for no relationship at all, and 100° for the closest possible relationship.

If no relationship should exist, there would nevertheless be a certain percentage of instances, due to pure chance, of the double event of whorls occurring in both ring-fingers, and it is easy to calculate their frequency from the above data. The number of possible combinations of 100 right ring-fingers with 100 left ones is 100×100, and of these 45×31 would be double events as above (call these for brevity "double whorls"). Consequently the chance of a double whorl in any single couplet is $\frac{45 \times 31}{100 \times 100}$, and their average frequency in 100 couplets,—in other words, their average percentage is $\frac{45 \times 31}{100} = 13.95$, say, 14. If, then, the observed percentage of double whorls should be only 14, it would be a proof that the A.L.W. classes of patterns on the right and left ring-fingers were quite independent; so their relationship, as expressed on the centesimal scale, would be 0°. There could never be less than 14 double whorls under the given conditions, except through some statistical irregularity.

Now consider the opposite extreme of the closest possible relationship, subject however, and this is the weak point, to the paramount condition that the average frequencies of the A.L.W. classes may be taken as *pre-established*. As there are 45 per cent of whorls on the right ring-finger, and only 31 on the left, the tendency to form double whorls, however stringent it may be, can only be satisfied in 31 cases. There remains a superfluity of 14 per cent cases in the right ring-finger which perforce must have for their partners either arches or loops. Hence the percentage of frequency that indicates the closest feasible relationship under the pre-established conditions, would be 31.

The range of all possible relationships in respect to whorls, would consequently lie between a percentage frequency of the minimum 14 and the maximum 31, while the observed frequency is of the intermediate value of 26. Subtracting the 14 from these three values, we have the series

of 0, 12, 17. These terms can be converted into their equivalents in a centesimal scale that reaches from 0° to 100° instead of from 0° to 17°, by
the ordinary rule of three, $12 : x : : 17 : 100$; $x = 70$ or 71, whence the
value x of the observed relationship on the centesimal scale would be 70°
or 71°, neglecting decimals.

This method of obtaining the value of 100° is open to grave objection
in the present example. We have no right to consider that the 45 per cent
of whorls on the right ring-finger, and the 31 on the left, can be due to pre-
established conditions, which would exercise a paramount effect even
though the whorls were due entirely to causes common to both fingers.
There is some self-contradiction in such a supposition. Neither are we at
liberty to assume that the respective effects of the special causes X and Z
are equal in average amount; if they were, the percentage of whorls on the
right and on the left finger would invariably be equal.

In this particular example the difficulty of determining correctly the
scale value of 100° is exceptionally great; elsewhere, the percentages of
frequency in the two members of each couplet are more alike. In the two
fore-fingers, and again in the two middle fingers, they are closely alike.
Therefore, in these latter cases, it is not unreasonable to pass over the
objection that X and Z have not been proved to be equal, but we must
accept the results in all other cases with great caution.

When the digits are of different names,—as the thumb and the fore-
finger,—whether the digits be on the same or on opposite hands, there are
two cases to be worked out; namely, such as (1) right thumb and left fore-
finger, and (2) left thumb and right fore-finger. Each accounts for 50 per
cent of the observed cases; therefore the mean of the two percentages is
the correct percentage. The relationships calculated in the following table
do not include arches, except in two instances mentioned in a subsequent
paragraph, as the arches are elsewhere too rare to furnish useful results.

It did not seem necessary to repeat the calculation for couplets of
digits of different names, situated on opposite hands, as those that were
calculated on closely the same data for similar couplets situated on the
same hands, suffice for both. It is evident from the irregularity in the run
of the figures that the units in the several entries cannot be more than
vaguely approximate. They have, however, been retained, as being possibly better than nothing at all.

TABLE VIII.

*Approximate Measures of Relationship between the various
Digits, on a Centesimal Scale.*

(0° = no relationship; 100° = the utmost feasible likeness.)

Couplets.	Loops.	Whorls.	Means.
Digits of same name.			
Right and left thumbs	57	64	61
" " fore-fingers	37	59	48
" " middle fingers	34	52	43
" " ring-fingers	61	70	65
Means.	47°	61°	54°
Digits of different names on the same or on opposite hands.			
Thumb and fore-finger	19	29	24
" middle finger	19	34	27
" ring finger	33	44	39
Fore and middle finger	52	68	60
" ring-finger	13	34	23
Middle and ring-finger	31	74	52
Means	28°	47°	37°

The arches were sufficiently numerous in the fore-fingers (17 per cent) to fully justify the application of this method of calculation. The result was 43°, which agrees fairly with 48°, the mean of the loops and the whorls. In the middle finger the frequency of the arches was only half the above amount and barely suffices for calculation. It gave the result of 38°, which also agrees fairly with 43°, the mean of the loops and the whorls for that finger.

Some definite results may be gathered from this table notwithstanding the irregularity with which the figures run. Its upper and lower halves clearly belong to different statistical groups, the entries in the former being almost uniformly larger than those in the latter, in the proportion of 54° to 37°, say 3 to 2, which roughly represents in numerical terms the nearer relationship between digits of the same name, as compared to that between digits of different names. It seems also that of the 6 couplets of digits bearing different names, the relationship is closest between the middle finger and the two adjacent ones (60° and 52°, as against 24°, 27°, 39° and 23°). It is further seen in every pair of entries that whorls are related together more closely than loops. I note this, but cannot explain it. So far as my statistical inquiries into heredity have hitherto gone, all peculiarities were found to follow the same law of transmission, none being more surely inherited than others. If there were a tendency in any one out of many alternative characters to be more heritable than the rest, that character would become universally prevalent, in the absence of restraining influences. But it does not follow that there are no peculiar restraining influences here, nor that what is true for heredity, should be true, in all its details, as regards the relationships between the different digits.

CHAPTER IX
METHODS OF INDEXING

In this chapter the system of classification by Arches, Loops, and Whorls described in Chapter V. will be used for indexing two, three, six or ten digits, as the case may be.

An index to each set of finger marks made by the same person, is needful in almost every kind of inquiry, whether it be for descriptive purposes, for investigations into race and heredity, or into questions of symmetry and correlation. It is essential to possess an index to the finger marks of known criminals before the method of finger prints can be utilised as an organised means of detection.

The ideal index might be conceived to consist of a considerable number of compartments, or their equivalents, each bearing a different index-heading, into which the sets of finger prints of different persons may be severally sorted, so that all similar sets shall lie in the same compartment.

The principle of the proposed method of index-headings is, that they should depend upon a few conspicuous differences of pattern in many fingers, and not upon many minute differences in a few fingers. It is carried into effect by distinguishing the A.L.W. class of pattern on each digit in succession, by a letter,—*a* for Arch, *l* for Loop, *w* for Whorl; or else, as an alternative method, to subdivide *l* by using *i* for a loop with an Inner slope, and *o* for one with an Outer slope, as the case may be. In this way, the class of pattern in each set of ten digits is described by a sequence of ten letters, the various combinations of which are alphabetically arranged and form the different index-headings. Let us now discuss the best method of carrying out this principle, by collating the results of alternative methods of applying it. We have to consider the utility of the *i* and *o* as compared to the simple *l*, and the gain through taking all ten digits into account, instead of only some of them.

TABLE IX. INDEX TO 100 SETS OF FINGER PRINTS.

Order of Entry	A Right F.M.R	B Left F.M.R.	C Right T.L.	D Left T.L.	Order of Entry	A Right F.M.R	B Left F.M.R.	C Right T.L.	D Left T.L.
1	aaa	aaa	aa	la	26	all	ill	wl	ll
2	"	"	al	al	27	"	oal	wl	ll
3	"	"	"	"	28	"	oll	wl	ll
4	"	"	wl	ll	29	"	www	wl	ll
5	aal	aal	al	al	30	alw	ilw	ll	ll
6	"	"	ll	ll	31	"	oal	ll	ll
7	"	"	"	"	32	"	oll	lw	ll
8	"	aaw	ll	ll	33	"	"	wl	wl
9	"	all	ll	ll	34	"	olw	al	al
10	"	"	lw	wl	35	ill	all	wl	ll
11	"	oll	ll	ll	36	"	"	wl	wl
12	aaw	aal	ll	ll	37	"	ill	ll	ll
13	"	all	ll	ll	38	"	"	"	"
14	ala	aaa	la	la	39	"	"	"	"
15	"	"	la	lw	40	"	"	"	"
16	"	oll	wl	ll	41	ill	ill	wl	ll
17	all	aal	ll	al	42	"	iww	wl	wl
18	"	"	ll	ll	43	ilw	ill	ll	wl
19	"	"	"	"	44	"	"	ww	wl
20	"	"	"	"	45	"	ilw	ww	wl
21	"	"	"	"	46	"	iwl	ll	ll
22	"	"	wl	ll	47	"	wlw	wl	wl
23	"	alw	ll	ll	48	"	wwl	ll	ll
24	"	ill	ll	ll	49	iww	all	wl	wl
25	"	"	"	"	50	"	www	wl	wl

It will be instructive to print here an actual index to the finger prints of 100 different persons, who were not in any way selected, but taken as they came, and to use it as the basis of a considerable portion of the following remarks, to be checked where necessary, by results derived from an index to 500 cases, in which these hundred are included.

This index is compiled on the principle shortly to be explained, entitled the "*i* and *o* fore-finger" method.

TABLE IX. INDEX TO 100 SETS OF FINGER PRINTS (continued).

Order of Entry	A Right F.M.R	B Left F.M.R.	C Right T.L.	D Left T.L.	Order of Entry	A Right F.M.R	B Left F.M.R.	C Right T.L.	D Left T.L.
51	"	www	wl	wl	76	wll	wll	ll	ll
52	oaw	oll	ll	ll	77	"	"	"	"
53	oll	all	wl	ll	78	"	"	"	"
54	"	"	"	"	79	"	"	wl	wl
55	"	"	"	"	80	"	wlw	ll	ll
56	"	"	wl	wl	81	wlw	olw	ll	ll
57	"	ill	ll	ll	82	"	"	ll	al
58	"	"	"	"	83	"	"	wl	ll
59	"	"	"	"	84	"	www	wl	wl
60	"	oll	ll	ll	85	"	"	ww	ll
61	"	"	"	"	86	"	"	ww	lw
62	"	"	"	"	87	"	"	ww	ww
63	"	"	"	"	88	"	"	"	"
64	"	"	"	"	89	wwl	ill	ll	ll
65	"	"	"	"	90	"	wll	wl	ll
66	"	wal	ll	wl	91	www	olw	wl	ll
67	"	www	ll	wl	92	"	wlw	wl	wl
68	olw	all	ll	ll	93	"	"	"	"
69	"	"	wl	wl	94	"	wwl	ll	lw
70	"	ill	wl	wl	95	"	www	il	ll
71	"	oll	ll	ll	96	"	"	wl	ll
72	"	olw	ll	ll	97	"	"	wl	wl
73	"	"	wl	ll	98	"	"	ww	wl
74	"	"	"	"	99	"	"	"	"
75	wll	ill	ll	wl	100	"	"	ww	ww

The sequence in which the digits have been registered is not from the thumb outwards to the little finger, but, on account of various good reasons that will be appreciated as we proceed, in the following order.

The ten digits are registered in four groups, which are distinguished in the Index by the letters A, B, C, D—

A. *First.* The fore, middle, and ring-fingers of the *right* hand taken in that order.

B. *Second.* The fore, middle, and ring-fingers of the *left* hand taken in that order.

C. *Third.* The thumb and little finger of the *right* hand.

D. *Fourth.* The thumb and little finger of the *left* hand.

Consequently an index-heading will be of the form—

First group.	Second group.	Third group.	Fourth group.
aal	*aaw*	*ll*	*ll*

These index-headings are catalogued in alphabetical order. The method used in the Index is that which takes note of no slopes, except those of loops in the fore-finger of either hand. Consequently the index-heading for my own digits, printed on the title-page, is *wlw oll wl wl*. Those of the eight sets in Plate VI. are as follows—

ilw	*ill*	*ww*	*wl*
olw	*olw*	*wl*	*ll*
olw	*oll*	*ll*	*ll*
ilw	*ilw*	*wl*	*wl*
ilw	*iwl*	*ll*	*ll*
ill	*wwl*	*ll*	*ll*
oll	*aal*	*ll*	*al*
oaa	*aaa*	*la*	*la*

For convenience of description and reference, the successive entries in the specimen index have been numbered from 1 to 100, but that is no part of the system: those figures would be replaced in a real index by names and addresses.

A preliminary way of obtaining an idea of the differentiating power of an index is to count the number of the different headings that are required to classify a specified number of cases. A table is appended which shows the numbers of the headings in the three alternative methods (1) of noting slopes of all kinds in all digits, (2) of noting slopes of Loops only and in the fore-fingers only, and (3) of disregarding the slopes altogether. Also in each of these three cases taking account of—

(*a*) All the ten digits;

(*b*) the fore, middle, and ring-fingers of both hands;

(*c*) those same three fingers, but of the right hand only;

(*d*) the fore and middle fingers of the right hand.

TABLE X.

No. of different index-heads in 100 *sets of Finger Prints.*

No. of digits regarded.	Digits noted.	Account taken of		
		All slopes.	*i* and *o* in fore-fingers.	No slope.
10	All the 10 digits	82	76	71
6 {	Fore, middle, and ring fingers of both hands ..	} 65	50	43
3	Of right hand only	25	16	14
2 {	Fore and middle of right hand only	} 12	8	7

The column headed "all slopes" refers to the method first used with success, and described in my Memoir, already alluded to (*Proc. Roy. Soc.*, 1891), accompanied by a specimen index, from which the present one was derived. There the direction of the slope of every pattern that has one, is taken into account, and in order to give as much scope as possible to the method, the term Arch (I then called it a Primary) was construed somewhat over-liberally (see p. 111). It was made to include the forked-arch Fig. 12 (2), and even the nascent-loop (9), so long as not more than a single recurved ridge lay within the outline of the pattern; therefore many of the so-called arches had slopes. It is not necessary to trouble the reader with the numerical nomenclature that was then used, the method itself being now obsolete. Full particulars of it are, however, given in the Memoir.

A somewhat large experience in sorting finger prints in various ways and repeatedly, made it only too evident that the mental strain and risk of error caused by taking all slopes into account was considerable. The judgment became fatigued and the eye puzzled by having to assign opposite meanings to the same actual direction of a slope in the right and left hands, respectively. There was also a frequent doubt as to the existence of a slope in large whorls of the spiral- and circlet-in-loop patterns (Fig. 13, 21, 22) when the impressions had not been rolled. A third objection is the rarity of the inner slopes in any other digit than the fore-finger. It acted like a soporific to the judgment not only of myself but of others, so that when an inner slope did occur it was apt to be overlooked. The first idea was to discard slopes altogether, notwithstanding the accompanying loss of index power, but this would be an unnecessarily trenchant measure. The slope of a loop, though it be on the fore-finger alone, decidedly merits recognition, for it differentiates such loops into two not very unequal classes. Again, there is little chance of mistake in noting it, the impression of the thumb on the one side and those of the remaining fingers on the other, affording easy guidance to the eye and judgment. These considerations determined the method I now use exclusively, by which Table IX. was compiled, and to which the second column of Table X., headed "i and o in fore-fingers," refers.

The heading of the third column, "no slope," explains itself, no account having been there taken of any slopes whatever, so i and o disappear, having become merged under l.

The table gives a very favourable impression of the differentiating power of all these methods of indexing. By the "i and o fore-finger" method, it requires as many as 76 different index-headings to include the finger prints of 100 different persons, 195 of 300 persons, and 285 of 500.

The number of entries under each index-heading varies greatly; reference to the index of 100 sets showing no less than six entries (Nos. 60–65) under one of them, and four entries (Nos. 18–21 and 37–40) under each of two others. Thus, although a large portion of the 100 sets are solitary entries under their several headings, and can be found by a single reference, the remainder are grouped together like the commoner surnames in a directory. They are troublesome to distinguish, and cannot be subdivided at all except by supplementary characteristics, such as the number of ridges in some specified part of the pattern, or the character of the cores.

In other respects the difference of merit between the three methods is somewhat greater, as is succinctly indicated by the next table.

TABLE XI. *In* 100 *Sets.*

Number of Entries under the same head.	No. of different index-headings.		
	All slopes.	*i* and *o* fore-fingers only.	No slope.
1	71	63	58
2	10	8	9
3	1	3	1
4	...	2	2
5	...	...	...
6	1	...	...
13	...	...	1
Total	83	76	71

Hence it is evident that the second method of "*i-o* fore-finger" is capable of dealing rapidly with 100 cases, but that the method of "no slope" will give trouble in twelve out of the hundred cases.

TABLE XII.

Index-headings under which more than 1 per cent of the sets of Finger Prints were registered.

(500 sets observed.)

No. for reference.	*i* and *o* in fore-fingers. Index-heading.				Frequency per cent.	No. for reference.	No slope. Index-heading.				Frequency per cent.
1	*all*	*all*	*ll*	*ll*	1.2	I.	*all*	*all*	*ll*	*ll*	1.2
2	*all*	*ill*	"	"	1.6	II.	*all*	*lll*	"	"	2.2
3	*ill*	*ill*	"	"	2.8						
4	*oll*	*ill*	"	"	1.4	III.	*lll*	*lll*	"	"	9.2
5	*oll*	*oll*	"	"	4.0						
6	*ill*	*oll*	*wl*	*ll*	1.2	IV.	*lll*	*lll*	*wl*	*ll*	3.2
7	*oll*	*oll*	"	"	1.4						
8	*oll*	*all*	*ll*	*ll*	2.2	V.	*lll*	*all*	*ll*	*ll*	3.0
9	*olw*	*ull*	"	"	2.0	VI.	*llw*	*lll*	"	"	3.0
10	*wll*	*wll*	"	"	1.2	VII.	*wll*	*wll*	"	"	1.2
11	*www*	*www*	*ww*	*ww*	1.4	VIII.	*www*	*www*	*ww*	*ww*	1.4

The headings in the right half of the table include more cases than the left half, because a combination of two or more cases that severally contain less than 1 per cent of the finger prints, and are therefore ignored in the first half of the table, may exceed 1 per cent and find a place in the second half.

The entries in Table XII. are derived from a catalogue of 500 sets, and include all entries that appeared more than five times; in other words, whose frequency exceeded 1 per cent. These are the index-headings that give enough trouble to deserve notice in catalogues of, say, from 500 to 1000 sets.

In the left half of Table XII. all the index-headings are given, under each of which more than 1 per cent of the sets fell, when the method of "*i* and *o* in fore-fingers" was adopted; also the respective percentage of the cases that fell under them. In the right half of the table are the corresponding index-headings, together with the percentages of frequency, when the "no slope" method is employed. These are distinguished by Roman numerals. The great advantage of the "*i* and *o* fore-finger" method lies in its power of breaking up certain large groups which are very troublesome to deal with by the "no slope" method. According to the latter as many as 9.2 per cent of all the entries fall under the index-heading marked III., but according to the "*i-o* fore-finger" method these are distributed among the headings 3, 4, and 5. The "all slopes" method has the peculiar merit of breaking up the large group Nos. 11 and VIII. of "all whorls," but its importance is not great on that account, as whorls are distinguishable by their cores, which are less troublesome to observe than their slopes.

The percentage of all the entries that fall under a single index-heading, according to the "*i-o* fore-finger" method, diminishes with the number of entries at the following rate—

TABLE XIII.

	Total number of entries.		
	100	300	500
Percentage of entries falling under a single head	63	49.0	39.8

It may be that every one of the $4^2 \times 3^8$, or one hundred and five thousand possible varieties of index-headings, according to the "*i-o* fore-finger" method, may occur in Nature, but there is much probability that some of them may be so rare that instances of no entry under certain heads would appear in the register, even of an enormous number of persons.

Hitherto we have supposed that prints of the ten fingers have in each case been indexed. The question now to be considered is the gain through dealing in each case with all ten digits, instead of following the easier practice of regarding only a few of them. The following table, drawn up from the hundred cases by the "all slopes" method, will show its amount.

TABLE XIV. *From* 100 *Sets.*

Digits.	No. of digits.	No. of different index-headings.		
		All slopes.	*i* and *o* fore-finger.	No slope.
Fore and middle of right hand	2	11	8	7
Fore, middle and ring of right hand	3	23	16	14
Fore, middle and ring of both hands	6	65	50	45
All ten digits	10	83	76	73

The trouble of printing, reading off, and indexing the ten digits, is practically twice that of dealing with the six fingers; namely, three on each of the hands; the thumb being inconvenient to print from, and having to be printed separately, even for a dabbed impression, while the fingers of either hand can be dabbed down simultaneously.

For a large collection the ten-digit method is certainly the best, as it breaks up the big battalions; also in case of one or more fingers having been injured, it gives reserve material to work upon.

We now come to the great difficulty in all classifications; that of transitional cases. What is to be done with those prints which cannot be certainly classed as Arches, Loops, or Whorls, but which lie between some two of them? These occur about once in every forty digits, or once in every four pairs of hands. The roughest way is to put a mark by the side of the entry to indicate doubt, a better one is to make a mark that shall express the nature of the peculiarity; thus a particular eyed pattern (Plate 10, Fig. 16, *n*) may be transitional between a loop and a whorl; under whichever of the two it is entered, the mark might be an *e* to show that anyhow it is an eye. Then, when it is required to discover whether an index contains a duplicate of a given specimen in which a transitional pattern occurs, the two headings between which the doubt lies have to be searched, and the marked entries will limit the search. Many alternative ways of marking may be successfully used, but I am not yet prepared to propose one as being distinctly the best. When there are two of these marks in the same set, it seldom happens that more than two references have to be made, as it is usual for the ambiguity to be of the same kind in both of the doubtful fingers. If the ambiguities were quite independent, then two marks would require four references, and three marks would require nine. There are a few nondescript prints that would fall under a separate heading, such as Z. Similarly, as regards lost or injured fingers.

I have tried various methods of sub-classification, and find no difficulty in any of them, but general rules seem inadvisable; it being best to treat each large group on its own merits.

One method that I have adopted and described in the *Proc. Royal Soc.*, is to sketch in a cursive and symbolic form the patterns of the several fingers in the order in which they appear in the print, confining myself to a limited number of symbols, such as might be used for printer's types. They sufficed fairly for some thousands of the finger marks upon which they were tried, but doubtless they could be improved. A little violence has of course to be used now and then, in fitting some unusual patterns to some one or other of these few symbols. But we are familiar with such processes in ordinary spelling, making the same letter do duty for different sounds, as *a* in the words *as*, *ale*, *ask*, and *all*. The plan of using symbols has many secondary merits. It facilitates a leisurely revision of first determinations, it affords a pictorial record of the final judgment that is directly comparable with the print itself, and it almost wholly checks blunders between inner and outer slopes. A beginner in finger reading will educate his judgment by habitually using them at first.

The cores give great assistance in breaking up the very large groups of all-loops (see Table XII., Nos. 11 and VIII.); so does an entry of the approximate number of ridges in some selected fingers, that lie between the core and the upper outline of the loop.

The plan I am now using for keeping finger prints in regular order, is this—In the principal collection, the prints of each person's ten digits are taken on the same large card; the four fingers of either hand being *dabbed* down simultaneously above, and all the ten digits *rolled* separately below. (Plate 2, Fig. 3.) Each card has a hole three-eighths of an inch in diameter, punched in the middle near to the bottom edge, and the cards are kept in trays, which they loosely fit, like the card catalogues used in many libraries. Each tray holds easily 500 cards, which are secured by a long stout wire passing like a skewer through the ends of the box and the holes in the cards. The hinder end of the box is sloped, so the cards can be tilted back and easily examined; they can be inserted or removed after withdrawing the wire.

It will be recollected that the leading and therefore the most conspicuous headings in the index refer to the fore, middle, and ring-fingers of the right hand, as entered in column A of the Specimen Register (Table IX.) The variety of these in the "*i* and *o* fore-finger" method, of which we are now speaking, cannot exceed thirty-six, there being only four varieties (*a, i, o, w*) in the fore-finger, and three varieties (*a, l, w*) in each of the other two; so their maximum number is $4 \times 3 \times 3 = 36$. The actual number of such index-headings in 500 cases, and the number of entries that fell under each, was found to be as follows—

TABLE XV.

No. of entries in 500 cases, under each of the thirty-six possible index-letters for the fore, middle, and ring-fingers of the right hand by the "i-o fore-finger" method.

aaa	4	iaa	1	oaa	1	waa	—
l	17	l	3	l	2	l	—
w	5	w	—	w	1	w	1
ala	3	ila	—	ola	2	wla	1
l	45	l	54	l	88	l	40
w	11	w	33	w	59	w	52
awa	—	iwa	—	owa	—	wwa	—
l	—	l	3	l	—	l	10
w	—	w	11	w	6	w	47

a = Arch.
i = Inward-sloped Loop on the fore-finger.
o = Outward-sloped Loop on the fore-finger.
l = Loop of either kind on the middle or ring finger.
w = Whorl.

These 500 cases supply no entries at all to eleven of the thirty-six index-headings, less than five entries (or under 1 per cent) to ten others, and the supply is distributed very unevenly among the remaining fifteen. This table makes it easy to calculate beforehand the spaces required for an index of any specified number of prints, whether they be on the pages of a Register, or in compartments, or in drawers of movable cards.

CHAPTER X
PERSONAL IDENTIFICATION

We shall speak in this chapter of the aid that finger prints can give to personal identification, supposing throughout that facilities exist for taking them well and cheaply, and that more or less practice in reading them has been acquired by many persons. A few introductory words will show this supposition to be reasonable. At the present moment any printer, and there are many printers in every town, would, at a small charge, blacken a slab and take the prints effectively, after being warned to use very little ink, as described in Chapter III. The occupation of finger printing would, however, fall more naturally into the hands of photographers, who, in addition to being found everywhere, are peculiarly well suited to it, for, taken as a class, they are naturally gifted with manual dexterity and mechanical ingenuity. Having secured good impressions, they could multiply them when necessary, and enlarge when desired, while the ticketing and preservation of the negatives would fall into their usual business routine. As they already occupy themselves with one means of identification, a second means of obtaining the same result is allied to their present work.

Were it the custom for persons about to travel to ask for prints of their fingers when they were photographed, a familiarity with the peculiarities of finger prints, and the methods of describing and classifying them, would become common. Wherever finger prints may be wanted for purposes of attestation and the like, the fact mentioned by Sir W. Herschel (p. 51) as to the readiness with which his native orderlies learnt to take them with the ink of his office stamp, must not be forgotten.

The remarks about to be made refer to identification generally, and are not affected by the fact that the complete process may or may not include the preliminary search of a catalogue; the two stages of search and of comparison will be treated separately towards the close of the chapter.

In civilised lands, honest citizens rarely need additional means of identification to their signatures, their photographs, and to personal introductions. The cases in which other evidence is wanted are chiefly connected with violent death through accident, murder, or suicide, which yield the constant and gruesome supply to the Morgue of Paris, and to corresponding institutions in other large towns, where the bodies of unknown persons are exposed for identification, often in vain. But when honest persons travel to distant countries where they have few or no friends, the need for a means of recognition is more frequently felt. The risk of death through accident or crime is increased, and the probability of subsequent identification diminished. There is a possibility not too remote to be disregarded, especially in times of war, of a harmless person being arrested by mistake for another man, and being in sore straits to give satisfactory proof of the error. A signature may be distrusted as a forgery. There is also some small chance, when he returns to his own country after a long absence, of finding difficulty in proving who he is. But in civilised lands and in peaceable times, the chief use of a sure means of identification is to benefit society by detecting rogues, rather than to establish the identity of men who are honest. Is this criminal an old offender? Is this new recruit a deserter? Is this professed pensioner personating a man who is dead? Is this upstart claimant to property the true heir, who was believed to have died in foreign lands?

In India and in many of our Colonies the absence of satisfactory means for identifying persons of other races is seriously felt. The natives are mostly unable to sign; their features are not readily distinguished by Europeans; and in too many cases they are characterised by a strange amount of litigiousness, wiliness, and unveracity. The experience of Sir W. Herschel, and the way in which he met these unfavourable conditions by the method of finger prints, has been briefly described in p. 38. Lately Major Ferris, of the Indian Staff Corps, happening to visit my laboratory during my absence, and knowing but little of what Sir W. Herschel had done, was greatly impressed by the possibilities of finger prints. After acquainting himself with the process, we discussed the subject together, and he very kindly gave me his views for insertion here. They are as follow, with a few trifling changes of words—

During a period of twenty-three years, eighteen of which have been passed in the Political Department of the Bombay Government, the great need of an official system of identification has been constantly forced on my mind.

The uniformity in the colour of hair, eyes, and complexion of the Indian races renders identification far from easy, and the difficulty of recording the description of an individual, so that he may be afterwards recognised, is very great. Again, their hand-writing, whether it be in Persian or Devanagri letters, is devoid of character and gives but little help towards identification.

The tenacity with which a native of India cleaves to his ancestral land, his innate desire to acquire more and more, and the obligation that accrues to him at birth of safeguarding that which has already been acquired, amounts to a religion, and passes the comprehension of the ordinary Western mind. This passion, or religion, coupled with a natural taste for litigation, brings annually into the Civil Courts an enormous number of suits affecting land. In a native State at one time under my political charge, the percentage of suits for the possession of land in which the title was disputed amounted to no less than 92, while in 83 per cent of these the writing by which the transfer of title purported to have been made, was repudiated by the former title-holder as fraudulent and not executed by him. When it is remembered that an enormous majority of the landholders whose titles come into court are absolutely illiterate, and that their execution of the documents is attested by a mark made by a third party, frequently, though not always apparently, interested in the transfer, it will be seen that there is a wide door open to fraud, whether by false repudiation or by criminal attempt at dispossession.

It has frequently happened in my experience that a transfer of title or possession was repudiated; the person purporting to have executed the transfer asserting that he had no knowledge of it, and never authorised any one to write, sign, or present it for registration. This was met by a categorical statement on the part of the beneficiary and of the attesting witnesses, concerning the time, date, and circumstances of the execution and registration, that demolished the simple denial of the man whom it was sought to dispossess. Without going into the ethics of falsehood among Western and Eastern peoples, it would be impossible to explain how what is repugnant to the one as downright lying, is very frequently considered as no more than venial prevarication by the other. This, however, is too large a subject for present purposes, but the fact remains that perjury is perpetrated in Indian Courts to an extent unknown in the United Kingdom.

The interests of landholders are partially safeguarded by the Act that requires all documents effecting the transfer of immovable property to be registered, but it could be explained, though not in the short space of this letter, how the provisions of the Act can be, and frequently are, fulfilled in the absence of the principal person, the executor.

Enough has been said to show that if some simple but efficient means could be contrived to identify the person who has executed a bond, cases of fraud such as these would practically disappear from the judicial registers. Were the legislature to amend the Registration Act and require that the original document as well as the copy in the Registration Book should bear the imprint of one or more fingers of the parties to the deed, I have little hesitation in saying that not only would fraud be detected, but that in a short time the facility of that detection would act as a deterrent for the future. [This was precisely the experience of Sir W. Herschel.—F.G.] In the majority of cases, the mere question would be, Is the man A the same person as B, or is he not? and of that question the finger marks would give unerring proof. For example, to take the simplest case, A is sued for possession of some land, the title of which he is stated to have parted with to another for a consideration. The document and the Registration Book both bear the imprint of the index finger of the right hand of A. A repudiates, and a comparison shows that whereas the finger pattern of A is a whorl, the imprint on the document is a loop; consequently A did not execute it.

In the identification of Government pensioners the finger print method would be very valuable. At one period, I had the payment of many hundreds of military pensioners. Personation was most difficult to detect in persons coming from a distance, who had no local acquaintances, and more especially where the claimants were women. The marks of identification noted in the pension roll were usually variations of—"Hair black—Eyes brown—Complexion wheat colour—Marks of tattooing on fore-arm"—terms which are equally appropriate to a large number of the pensioners. The description was supplemented in some instances, where the pensioner had some distinguishing mark or scar, but such cases are considerably rarer than might be supposed, and in women the marks are not infrequently in such a position as to practically preclude comparison. Here also the imprint of one or more finger prints on the pension certificate, would be sufficient to settle any doubt as to identity.

As a large number of persons pass through the Indian gaols not only while undergoing terms of imprisonment, but in default of payment of a fine, it could not but prove of value were the finger prints of one and all secured. They might assist in identifying persons who have formerly been convicted, of whom the local police have no knowledge, and who bear a name that may be the common property of half a hundred in any small town.

Whatever difficulty may be felt in the identification of Hindoos, is experienced in at least an equal degree in that of the Chinese residents in our Colonies and Settlements, who to European eyes are still more alike than the Hindoos, and in whose names there is still less variety. I have already referred (p. 38) to Mr. Tabor, of San Francisco, and his proposal in respect to the registration of the Chinese. Remarks showing the need of some satisfactory method of identifying them, have reached me from various sources. The *British North Borneo Herald*, August 1, 1888, that lies before me as I write, alludes to the difficulty of identifying coolies, either by photographs or measurements, as likely to become important in the early future of that country.

For purposes of registration, the method of printing to be employed, must be one that gives little trouble on the one hand, and yields the maximum of efficiency for that amount of trouble on the other. Sir W. Herschel impressed simultaneously the fore and middle fingers of the right hand. To impress simultaneously the fore, middle, and ring-fingers of the right hand ought, however, to be better, the trouble being no greater, while three prints are obviously more effective than two, especially for an off-hand comparison. Moreover, the patterns on the ring-finger are much more variable than those on the middle finger. Much as rolled impressions are to be preferred for minute and exhaustive comparisons, they would probably be inconvenient for purposes of registration or attestation. Each finger has to be rolled separately, and each separate rolling takes more time than a dab of all the fingers of one hand simultaneously. Now a dabbed impression of even two fingers is more useful for registration purposes than the rolled impression of one; much more is a dabbed impression of three, especially when the third is the variable ring-finger. Again, in a simultaneous impression, there is no doubt as to the sequence of the finger prints being correct, but there may be some occasional bungling when the fingers are printed separately.

For most criminal investigations, and for some other purposes also, the question is not the simple one just considered, namely, "Is A the same person, or a different person from B?" but the much more difficult problem of "Who is this unknown person X? Is his name contained in such and such a register?" We will now consider how this question may be answered.

Registers of criminals are kept in all civilised countries, but in France they are indexed according to the method of M. Alphonse Bertillon, which admits of an effective search being made through a large collection. We shall see how much the differentiating power of the French or of any other system of indexing might be increased by including finger prints in the register.

M. Bertillon has described his system in three pamphlets—

(1) *Une application pratique de l'anthropometrie*, Extrait des Annales de Démographie Interne. Paris 1881. (2) *Les signalements anthropometriques*, Conference faite au Congrès Penitentiare International de Rome, Nov. 22, 1885. (3) *Sur le fonctionnement du service des signalements*. All the above are published by Masson, 120 Boulevard St. Germain, Paris. To these must be added a very interesting but anonymous pamphlet, based on official documents, and which I have reason to know is authorised by M. Bertillon, namely, (4) *L'anthropometrie Judiciare en Paris, en* 1889: G. Stenheil, 2 Rue Casimir-Delavigne, Paris.

Besides these a substantial volume is forthcoming, which may give a satisfactory solution to some present uncertainties.

The scale on which the service is carried on, is very large. It was begun in 1883, and by the end of 1887 no less than 60,000 sets of measures were in hand, but thus far only about one half of the persons arrested in Paris were measured, owing to the insufficiency of the staff. Arrangements were then made for its further extension. There are from 100 to 150 prisoners sentenced each day by the Courts of Law in Paris to more than a few days' imprisonment, and every one of these is sent to the Dépôt for twenty-four hours. While there, they are now submitted to *Bertillonage*, a newly coined word that has already come into use. This is done in the forenoon, by three operators and three clerks; six officials in all. About half of the prisoners are old offenders, of whom a considerable proportion give their names correctly, as is rapidly verified by an alphabetically arranged catalogue of cards, each of which contains front and profile photographs, and measurements. The remainder are examined strictly; their bodily marks are recorded according to a terse system of a few letters, and they are variously measured. Each person occupies seven or eight minutes. They are then photographed. From sixty to seventy-five prisoners go through this complete process every forenoon. In the afternoon the officials are engaged in making numerous copies of each set of records, one of which is sent to Lyon, and another to Marseille, where there are similar establishments. They also classify the copies of records that are received from those towns and elsewhere in France, of which from seventy to one hundred arrive daily. Lastly, they search the Registers for duplicate sets of measures of those, whether in Paris or in the provinces, who were suspected of having given false names. The entire staff consists of ten persons. It is difficult to rightly interpret the figures given in the pamphlet (4) at pp. 22–24, as they appear to disagree, but as I understand them, 562 prisoners who gave false names in the year 1890 were recognised by *Bertillonage*, and only four other persons were otherwise discovered to have been convicted previously, who had escaped recognition by its means.

I had the pleasure of seeing the system in operation in Paris a few years ago, and was greatly impressed by the deftness of the measuring, and with the swiftness and success with which the assistants searched for the cards containing entries similar to the measures of the prisoner then under examination.

It is stated in the *Signalements* (p. 12) that the basis of the classification are the four measurements (1) Head-length, (2) Head-breadth, (3) Middle-finger-length, (4) Foot-length, their constancy during adult life nearly always [as stated] holding good. Each of these four elements severally is considered as belonging to one or other of three equally numerous classes—small, medium, and large; consequently there are 3^4 or 81 principal headings, under some one of which the card of each prisoner is in the first instance sorted. Each of these primary headings is successively subdivided, on the same general principle of a three-fold classification, according to other measures that are more or less subject to uncertainties, namely, the height, the span, the cubit, the length and breadth of the ear, and the height of the bust. The eye-colour alone is subjected to seven divisions. The general result is (pp. 19, 22) that a total of twelve measures are employed, of which eleven are classed on the three-fold principle, and one on the seven-fold, giving a final result of $3^{11} \times 7$, or more than a million possible combinations. M. Bertillon considers it by no means necessary to stop here, but in his chapter (p. 22) on the "Infinite Extension of the Classification," claims that the method may be indefinitely extended.

The success of the system is considered by many experts to be fully proved, notwithstanding many apparent objections, one of which is the difficulty due to transitional cases: a belief in its success has certainly obtained a firm hold upon the popular imagination in France. Its general acceptance elsewhere seems to have been delayed in part by a theoretical error in the published calculations of its efficiency: the measures of the limbs which are undoubtedly correlated being treated as independent, and in part by the absence of a sufficiently detailed account of the practical difficulties experienced in its employment. Thus in the *Application pratique*, p. 9: "We are embarrassed what to choose, the number of human measures which vary independently of each other being considerable." In the *Signalements*, p. 19: "It has been shown" (by assuming this independent variability) "that by seven measurements, 60,000 photographs can be separated into batches of less than ten in each." (By the way, even on that assumption, the result is somewhat exaggerated, the figures having been arrived at by successively taking the higher of the two nearest round values.) In short, the general tone of these two memoirs is one of enthusiastic belief in the method, based almost wholly, so far as is there shown, on questionable *theoretic* grounds of efficiency.

To learn how far correlation interferes with the regularity of distribution, causing more entries to be made under some index-heads than others, as was the case with finger prints, I have classified on the Bertillon system, 500 sets of measures taken at my laboratory. It was not practicable to take more than three of the four primary measures, namely, the headlength, its breadth, and the middle-finger-length. The other measure, that of foot-length, is not made at my laboratory, as it would require the shoes to be taken off, which is inconvenient since persons of all ranks and both sexes are measured there; but this matters little for the purpose immediately in view. It should, however, be noted that the head-length and head-breadth have especial importance, being only slightly correlated, either together or with any other dimension of the body. Many a small man has a head that is large in one or both directions, while a small man rarely has a large foot, finger, or cubit, and conversely with respect to large men.

The following set of five measures of each of the 500 persons were then tabulated: (1) head-length; (2) head-breadth; (3) span; (4) body-height, that is the height of the top of the head from the seat on which the person sits; (5) middle-finger-length. The measurements were to the nearest tenth of an inch, but in cases of doubt, half-tenths were recorded in (1), (2), and (5). With this moderate minuteness of measurement, it was impossible so to divide the measures as to give better results than the following, which show that the numbers in the three classes are not as equal as desirable. But they nevertheless enable us to arrive at an approximate idea of the irregular character of the distribution.

TABLE XVI.

Dimensions measured.	Medium measures in inches and tenths.	Nos. in the three classes, respectively.			
		− below.	0 medium.	+ above.	Total.
1. Head-length	7.5 to 7.7	101	191	208	500
2. Head-breadth	6.0 „ 6.1	173	201	126	500
3. Span	68.0 „ 70.5	137	165	198	500
4. Body-height	35.0 „ 36.0	139	168	193	500
5. Middle-finger	4.5 „ 4.6	180	176	144	500

The distribution of the measures is shown in Table XVII.

TABLE XVII.

Distribution of 500 sets of measures into classes. Each set consists of five elements; each element is classed as + or above medium class; M, or mediocre; –, or below medium class.

(Total number of classes is 3^5 = 243.)

3 Span.	4 Body-height.	5 Middle-finger.	1 Head-length, 2 Head-breadth.								
			1 2	1 2	1 2	1 2	1 2	1 2	1 2	1 2	1 2
			– –	– M	– +	M –	M M	M +	+ –	+ M	+ +
–	–	–	14	7	4	14	11	5	3	3	2
		M	–	2	–	2	4	1	–	2	4
		+	–	–	–	1	–	–	–	–	–
–	M	–	5	2	2	7	4	2	1	4	3
		M	–	2	–	3	1	3	2	3	–
		+	–	–	–	–	–	–	–	–	2
–	+	–	2	–	–	1	1	1	–	–	1
		M	–	2	–	–	–	–	–	1	1
		+	–	–	–	1	–	–	–	1	–
M	–	–	4	–	1	3	4	3	1	2	2
		M	3	2	–	3	2	3	2	4	–
		+	–	–	–	–	1	2	–	1	–
M	M	–	1	3	1	4	3	2	4	4	3
		M	5	3	–	7	5	2	2	6	5
		+	2	1	1	1	1	–	1	4	2
M	+	–	2	1	1	5	2	–	–	2	2
		M	2	2	–	3	3	1	1	6	7
		+	–	–	1	2	–	–	3	2	2
+	–	–	–	–	1	–	1	–	–	–	–
		M	1	–	–	1	2	–	1	3	–
		+	1	2	–	1	1	–	–	–	2
+	M	–	1	–	1	3	2	–	–	–	2
		M	2	–	1	1	4	–	3	2	4
		+	2	1	–	2	4	1	4	6	3
+	+	–	1	2	–	1	–	1	1	2	2
		M	–	1	–	5	10	3	3	8	9
		+	2	2	2	11	10	3	9	24	19

The frequency with which 1, 2, 3, 4, etc., sets were found to fall under the same index-heading, is shown in Table XVIII.

TABLE XVIII.

No. of sets under same index-heading.	Frequency of its occurrence.	No. of entries.
0	83	0
1	47	47
2	47	94
3	25	75
4	16	64
5	7	35
6	3	18
7	4	28
8	1	8
9	2	18
10	2	20
11	2	22
14	2	28
19	1	19
24	1	24
Total entries 500		

No example was found of 83, say of one-third, of the 243 possible combinations. In one case no less than 24 sets fell under the same head; in another case 19 did so, and there were two cases in which 14, 11, and 10 severally did the same. Thus, out of 500 sets (see the five bottom lines in the last column of the above table) no less than 113 sets fell into four classes, each of which included from 10 to 24 entries.

The 24 sets whose index-number is +M, + + + admit of being easily subdivided and rapidly sorted by an expert, into smaller groups, paying regard to considerable differences only, in the head-length and head-breadth. After doing this, two comparatively large groups remain, with five cases in each, which require further analysis. They are as follow, the height and eye-colour being added in each case, and brackets being so placed as to indicate measures that do not differ to a sufficient amount to be surely distinguished. No two sets are alike throughout, some difference of considerable magnitude always occurring to distinguish them. Nos. 2 and 3 come closest together, and are distinguished by eye-colour alone.

TABLE XIX.

Five cases of Head-length 8.0, and Head-breadth 6.1.

	Span.	Body.	Finger.	Height.	Eye-colour.
1.	72.4	38.0	4.8	71.2	br. grey
2.	72.6	37.0	4.7	71.4	br. grey
3.	72.7	36.7	4.7	71.4	blue
4.	73.9	36.4	5.0	70.7	brown
5.	75.3	37.9	4.8	73.4	blue

Five cases of Head-length 7.8, and Head-breadth 6.0.

	Span.	Body.	Finger.	Height.	Eye-colour.
6.	70.8	37.8	4.7	70.0	brown
7.	71.9	36.2	4.7	69.3	blue
8.	72.4	37.2	4.7	68.4	brown
9.	74.8	37.8	5.0	73.1	blue
10.	79.9	37.3	5.3	75.6	blue grey

This is satisfactory. It shows that each one of the 500 sets may be distinguished from all the others by means of only seven elements; for if it is possible so to subdivide twenty-four entries that come under one index-heading, we may assume that we could do so in the other cases where the entries were fewer. The other measures that I possess—strength of grasp and breathing capacity—are closely correlated with stature and bulk, while eyesight and reaction-time are uncorrelated, but the latter are hardly suited to test the further application of the Bertillon method.

It would appear, from these and other data, that a purely anthropometric classification, irrespective of bodily marks and photographs, would enable an expert to deal with registers of considerable size.

Bearing in mind that mediocrities differ less from one another than members of either of the extreme classes, and would therefore be more difficult to distinguish, it seems probable that with comparatively few exceptions, *at least* two thousand adults of the same sex might be individualised, merely by means of twelve careful measures, on the Bertillon system, making reasonable allowances for that small change of proportions that occurs after the lapse of a few years, and for inaccuracies of measurement. This estimate may be far below the truth, but more cannot, I think, be safely inferred from the above very limited experiment.

The system of registration adopted in the American army for tracing suspected deserters, was described in a memoir contributed to the "International Congress of Demography," held in London in 1891. The memoir has so far been only published in the *Abstracts of Papers*, p. 233 (Eyre and Spottiswoode). Its phraseology is unfortunately so curt as sometimes to be difficult to understand; it runs as follows—

Personal identity as determined by scars and other body marks by Colonel Charles R. Greenleaf and Major Charles Smart, Medical Department, U.S. Army.

Desertions from United States army believed to greatly exceed deserters, owing to repeaters.

Detection of repeaters possible if all body marks of all recruits recorded, all deserters noted, and all recruits compared with previous deserters.

In like manner men discharged for cause excluded from reentry.

Bertillon's anthropometric method insufficient before courts-martial, because possible inaccuracies in measurement, and because of allowable errors.

But identity acknowledged following coincident indelible marks, when height, age, and hair fairly correspond.

That is, Bertillon's collateral evidence is practically primary evidence for such purposes.

There is used for each man an outline figure card giving anterior and posterior surfaces, divided by dotted lines into regions.

These, showing each permanent mark, are filed alphabetically at the Surgeon-General's office, War Department.

As a man goes out for cause, or deserts, his card is placed in a separate file.

The cards of recruits are compared with the last-mentioned file.

To make this comparison, a register in two volumes is opened, one for light-eyed and one for dark-eyed men. Each is subdivided into a fair number of pages, according to height of entrants, and each page is ruled in columns for body regions. Tattooed and non-tattooed men of similar height and eyes are entered on opposite pages. Recruits without tattoos are not compared with deserters with tattoos; but recruits with tattoos are compared with both classes.

On the register S T B M, etc., are used as abbreviations for scar, tattoo, birth-mark, mole, etc.

One inch each side of recorded height allowed for variation or defective measurement.

When probability of identity appears, the original card is used for comparison.

Owing to obstacles in inaugurating new system, its practical working began with 1891, and, to include May 1891 [= 5 months, F.G.], out of sixty-two cases of suspected fraud sixty-one proved real.

There was some interesting discussion, both upon this memoir and on a verbal communication concerning the French method, that had been made by M. Jacques Bertillon the statistician, who is a brother of its originator. It appeared that there was room for doubt whether the anthropometric method had received a fair trial in America, the measurements being made by persons not specially trained, whereas in France the establishments, though small, are thoroughly efficient.

There are almost always moles or birth-marks, serving for identification, on the body of every one, and a record of these is, as already noted, an important though subsidiary part of the Bertillon system. Body-marks are noted in the English registers of criminals, and it is curious how large a proportion of these men are tattooed and scarred. How far the body-marks admit of being usefully charted on the American plan, it is difficult to say, the success of the method being largely dependent on the care with which they are recorded. The number of persons hitherto dealt with on the American plan appears not to be very large. As observations of this class require the person to be undressed, they are unsuitable for popular purposes of identification, but the marks have the merit of serving to identify at all ages, which the measurements of the limbs have not.

It seems strange that no register of this kind, so far as I know, takes account of the teeth. If a man, on being first registered, is deficient in certain teeth, they are sure to be absent when he is examined on a future occasion. He may, and probably will in the meantime, have lost others, but the fact of his being without specified teeth on the first occasion, excludes the possibility of his being afterwards mistaken for a man who still possesses them.

We will now separately summarise the results arrived at, in respect to the two processes that may both be needed in order to effect an identification.

First, as regards *search in an Index*. Some sets of measures will give trouble, but the greater proportion can apparently be catalogued with so much certainty, that if a second set of measures of any individual be afterwards taken, no tedious search will be needed to hunt out the former set. Including the bodily marks and photographs, let us rate the Bertillon method as able to cope with a register of 20,000 adults of the same sex, with a small and definable, but as yet unknown, average dose of difficulty, which we will call x.

A catalogue of 500 sets of finger prints easily fulfils the same conditions. I could lay a fair claim to much more, but am content with this. Now the finger patterns have been shown to be so independent of other conditions that they cannot be notably, if at all, correlated with the bodily measurements or with any other feature, not the slightest trace of any relation between them having yet been found, as will be shown at p. 166, and more fully in Chapter XII. For instance, it would be totally impossible to fail to distinguish between the finger prints of twins, who in other respects appeared exactly alike. Finger prints may therefore be treated without the fear of any sensible error, as varying quite independently of the measures and records in the Bertillon system. Their inclusion would consequently increase its power fully five-hundred fold. Suppose one moderate dose of difficulty, x, is enough for dealing with the measurements, etc., of 20,000 adult persons of the same sex by the Bertillon method, and a similar dose of difficulty with the finger prints of 500 persons, then two such doses could deal with a register of 20,000 × 500, or 10,000,000.

We now proceed to consider the second and final process, namely, that of identification by *Comparison*. When the data concerning a suspected person are discovered to bear a general likeness to one of those already on the register, and a minute comparison shows their finger prints to agree in all or nearly all particulars, the evidence thereby afforded that they were made by the same person, far transcends in trustworthiness any other evidence that can ordinarily be obtained, and vastly exceeds all that can be derived from any number of ordinary anthropometric data. *By itself it is amply sufficient to convict.* Bertillonage can rarely supply more than grounds for very strong suspicion: the method of finger prints affords certainty. It is easy, however, to understand that so long as the peculiarities of finger prints are not generally understood, a juryman would be cautious in accepting their evidence, but it is to be hoped that attention will now gradually become drawn to their marvellous virtues, and that after their value shall have been established in a few conspicuous cases, it will come to be popularly recognised.

Let us not forget two great and peculiar merits of finger prints; they are self-signatures, free from all possibility of faults in observation or of clerical error; and they apply throughout life.

An abstract of the remarks made by M. Herbette, Director of the Penitentiary Department of the Ministère de l'Intérieur, France, at the International Penitentiary Congress at Rome, after the communication by M. Alphonse Bertillon had been read, may fitly follow.

> Proceeding to a more extended view of the subject and praising the successful efforts of M. Bertillon, M. Herbette pointed out how a verification of the physical personality, and of the identity of people of adult age, would fulfil requirements of modern society in an indisputable manner under very varied conditions.
>
> If it were a question, for instance, of giving to the inhabitants of a country, to the soldiers of an army, or to travellers proceeding to distant lands, notices or personal cards as recognisable signs, enabling them

always to prove who they are; if it were a question of completing the obligatory records of civil life by perfectly sure indications, such as would prevent all error, or substitution of persons; if it were a question of recording the distinctive marks of an individual in documents, titles or contracts, where his identity requires to be established for his own interest, for that of third parties, or for that of the State,—there the anthropometric system of identification would find place.

Should it be a question of a life certificate, of a life assurance, or of a proof of death, or should it be required to certify the identity of a person who was insane, severely wounded, or of a dead body that had been partly destroyed, or so disfigured as to be hardly recognisable from a sudden or violent death due to crime, accident, shipwreck, or battle—how great would be the advantage of being able to trace these characters, unchangeable as they are in each individual, infinitely variable as between one individual and another, indelible, at least in part, even in death.

There is still more cause to be interested in this subject when it is a question of identifying persons who are living at a great distance, and after the lapse of a considerable time, when the physiognomy, the features, and the physical habits may have changed from natural or artificial causes, and to be able to identify them without taking a journey and without cost, by the simple exchange of a few lines or figures that may be sent from one country or continent to another, so as to give information in America as to who any particular man is, who has just arrived from France, and to certify whether a certain traveller found in Rome is the same person who was measured in Stockholm ten years before.

In one word, to fix the human personality, to give to each human being an identity, an individuality that can be depended upon with certainty, lasting, unchangeable, always recognisable and easily adduced, this appears to be in the largest sense the aim of the new method.

Consequently, it may be said that the extent of the problem, as well as the importance of its solution, far exceeds the limits of penitentiary work and the interest, which is however by no means inconsiderable, that penal action has excited amongst various nations. These are the motives for giving to the labours of M. Bertillon and to their practical utilisation the publicity they merit.

These full and clear remarks seem even more applicable to the method of finger prints than to that of anthropometry.

CHAPTER XI
HEREDITY

Some of those who have written on finger marks affirm that they are transmissible by descent, others assert the direct contrary, but no inquiry hitherto appears to justify a definite conclusion.

Chapter VIII shows a close correlation to exist between the patterns on the several fingers of the same person. Hence we are justified in assuming that the patterns are partly dependent on constitutional causes, in which case it would indeed be strange if the general law of heredity failed in this particular case.

After examining many prints, the frequency with which some peculiar pattern was found to characterise members of the same family convinced me of the reality of an hereditary tendency. The question was how to submit the belief to numerical tests; particular kinships had to be selected, and methods of discussion devised.

It must here be borne in mind that "Heredity" implies more than its original meaning of a relationship between parent and child. It includes that which connects children of the same parents, and which I have shown (*Natural Inheritance*) to be just twice as close in the case of stature as that which connects a child and either of its two parents. Moreover, the closeness of the fraternal and the filial relations are to a great extent interdependent, for in any population whose faculties remain *statistically* the same during successive generations, it has been shown that a simple algebraical equation must exist, that connects together the three elements of Filial Relation, Fraternal Relation, and Regression, by which a knowledge of any two of them determines the value of the third. So far as

Regression may be treated as being constant in value, the Filial and the Fraternal relations become reciprocally connected. It is not possible briefly to give an adequate explanation of all this now, or to show how strictly observations were found to confirm the theory; this has been fully done in *Natural Inheritance*, and the conclusions will here be assumed.

The fraternal relation, besides disclosing more readily than other kinships the existence or non-existence of heredity, is at the same time more convenient, because it is easier to obtain examples of brothers and sisters alone, than with the addition of their father and mother. The resemblance between those who are twins is also an especially significant branch of the fraternal relationship. The word "fraternities" will be used to include the children of both sexes who are born of the same parents; it being impossible to name the familiar kinship in question either in English, French, Latin, or Greek, without circumlocution or using an incorrect word, thus affording a striking example of the way in which abstract thought outruns language, and its expression is hampered by the inadequacy of language. In this dilemma I prefer to fall upon the second horn, that of incorrectness of phraseology, subject to the foregoing explanation and definition.

The first preliminary experiments were made with the help of the Arch–Loop–Whorl classification, on the same principle as that already described and utilised in Chapter VIII., with the following addition. Each of the two members of any couplet of fingers has a distinctive name—for instance, the couplet may consist of a finger and a thumb; or again, if it should consist of two fore-fingers, one will be a right fore-finger and the other a left one, but the two brothers in a couplet of brothers rank equally as such. The plan was therefore adopted of "ear-marking" the prints of the first of the two brothers that happened to come to hand, with an A, and that of the second brother with a B; and so reducing the questions to the shape—How often does the pattern on the finger of a B brother agree with that on the corresponding finger of an A brother? How often would it occur between two persons who had no family likeness? How often would it correspond if the kinship between A and B were as close as it is possible to conceive? Or transposing the questions, and using the same words as in Chapter VIII., what is the relative frequency of (1) Random occurrences, (2) Observed occurrences, (3) Utmost possibilities? It was shown in that chapter how to find the value of (2) upon a centesimal scale in which "Randoms" ranked as 0° and "Utmost possibilities" as 100°.

The method there used of calculating the frequency of the "Random" events will be accepted without hesitation by all who are acquainted with the theory and the practice of problems of probability. Still, it is as well to occasionally submit calculation to test. The following example was sent to me for that purpose by a friend who, not being mathematically minded, had demurred somewhat to the possibility of utilising the calculated "Randoms."

The prints of 101 (by mistake for 100) couplets of prints of the right fore-fingers of school children were taken by him from a large collection, the two members, A and B, being picked out at random and formed into a couplet. It was found that among the A children there were 22 arches, 50 loops, and 29 whorls, and among the B children 25, 34, and 42 respectively, as is shown by the *italic* numerals in the last column, and again in the bottom row of Table XX. The remainder of the table shows the number of times in which an arch, loop, or whorl of an A child was associated with an arch, loop, or whorl of a B child.

TABLE XX.
Observed Random Couplets.

B children.	A children.			Totals in B children.
	Arches.	Loops.	Whorls.	
Arches	5	12	82	25
Loops	8	18	8	34
Whorls	9	20	13	42
Totals in A children	22	50	29	101

TABLE XXI.
Calculated Random Couplets.

B children.	A children.			Totals in B children.
	Arches.	Loops.	Whorls.	
Arches	5.00	12.50	7.25	25
Loops	6.80	17.00	9.86	34
Whorls	8.40	21.00	12.18	42
Totals in A children	22	50	29	101

The question, then, was how far calculations from the above data would correspond with the contents of Table XX. The answer is that it does so admirably. Multiply each of the italicised A totals into each of the italicised B totals, and after dividing each result by 101, enter it in the square at which the column that has the A total at its base, is intersected by the row that has the B total at its side. We thus obtain Table XXI.

We will now discuss in order the following relationships: the Fraternal, first in the ordinary sense, and then in the special case of twins of the same set; Filial, in the special case in which both parents have the same particular pattern on the same finger; lastly, the relative influence of the father and mother in transmitting their patterns.

Fraternal relationship. In 105 fraternities the *observed* figures were as in Table XXII—

TABLE XXII.
Observed Fraternal Couplets.

B children.	A children.			Totals in B children.
	Arches.	Loops.	Whorls.	
Arches.	5	12	2	19
Loops.	4	42	15	61
Whorls.	1	14	10	25
Totals in A children	10	68	27	105

The squares that run diagonally from the top at the left, to the bottom at the right, contain the double events, and it is with these that we are now concerned. Are the entries in those squares larger or not than the randoms, calculated as above, viz., the values of 10×19, 68×61, 27×25, all divided by 105? The calculated Randoms are shown in the first line of Table XXIII., the third line gives the greatest feasible number of correspondences which would occur if the kinship were as close as possible, subject to the reservation explained in p. 121. As there shown, the *lower* of the A and B values is taken in each case, for Arches, Loops, and Whorls, respectively.

TABLE XXIII.

	A and B both being		
	Arches.	Loops.	Whorls.
Random	1.7	37.6	6.2
Observed	5.0	42.0	10.0
Utmost feasible	10.0	61.0	25.0

In every instance, the Observed values are seen to exceed the Random.

Many other cases of this description were calculated, all yielding the same general result, but these results are not as satisfactory as can be wished, owing to their dilution by inappropriate cases, the A.L.W. system being somewhat artificial.

With the view of obtaining a more satisfactory result the patterns were subdivided under fifty-three heads, and an experiment was made with the fore, middle, and ring-fingers of 150 fraternal couplets (300 individuals and 900 digits) by Mr. F. Howard Collins, who kindly undertook the considerable labour of indexing and tabulating them.

The provisional list of standard patterns published in the *Phil. Trans.* was not appropriate for this purpose. It related chiefly to thumbs, and consequently omitted the tented arch; it also referred to the left hand, but in the following tabulations the right hand has been used; and its numbering is rather inconvenient. The present set of fifty-three patterns has faults, and cannot be considered in any way as final, but it was suitable for our purposes and may be convenient to others; as Mr. Collins worked wholly by it, it may be distinguished as the "C. set." The banded patterns, 24–31, are very rarely found on the fingers, but being common on the thumb, were retained, on the chance of our requiring the introduction of thumb patterns into the tabulations. The numerals refer to the patterns as seen in impressions of the *right hand* only. [They would be equally true for the patterns as seen on the *fingers themselves* of the left hand.] For impressions of the left hand the numerals up to 7 inclusive would be the same, but those of all the rest would be changed. These are arranged in couplets, the one member of the couplet being a reversed picture of the other, those in each couplet being distinguished by severally bearing an odd and an even number. Therefore, in impressions of the left hand, 8 would have to be changed into 9, and 9 into 8; 10 into 11, and 11 into 10; and so on, up to the end, viz., 52 and 53. The numeral 54 was used to express nondescript patterns.

The finger prints had to be gone through repeatedly, some weeks elapsing between the inspections, and under conditions which excluded the possibility of unconscious bias; a subject of frequent communication between Mr. Collins and myself. Living at a distance apart, it was not easy at the time they were made, to bring our respective interpretations of transitional and of some of the other patterns, especially the invaded loops, into strict accordance, so I prefer to keep his work, in which I have perfect confidence, independent from my own. Whenever a fraternity consisted of more than two members, they were divided, according to a prearranged system, into as many couplets as there were individuals. Thus, while a fraternity of three individuals furnished all of its three possible varieties of couplets, (1, 2), (1, 3), (2, 3), one of four individuals was not allowed to furnish more than four of its possible couplets, the two italicised ones being omitted, (1, 2), (1, 3), (*1, 4*), (2, 3), (2, 4), (3, 4), and so on. Without this precaution, a single very large family might exercise a disproportionate and even overwhelming statistical influence.

It would be essential to exact working, that the mutual relations of the patterns should be taken into account; for example, suppose an arch to be found on the fore-finger of one brother and a nascent loop on that of the other; then, as these patterns are evidently related, their concurrence ought to be interpreted as showing some degree of resemblance. However, it was impossible to take cognizance of partial resemblances, the mutual relations of the patterns not having, as yet, been determined with adequate accuracy.

The completed tabulations occupied three large sheets, one for each of the fingers, ruled crossways into fifty-three vertical columns for the A brothers, and fifty-three horizontal rows for the B brothers. Thus, if the register number of the pattern of A was 10, and that of B was 42, then a mark would be put in the square limited by the ninth and tenth horizontal lines, and by the forty-first and forty-second vertical ones. The marks were scattered sparsely over the sheet. Those in each square were then added up, and finally the numbers in each of the rows and in each of the columns were severally totalled.

If the number of couplets had been much greater than they are, a test of the accuracy with which their patterns had been classed under the appropriate heads, would be found in the frequency with which the same patterns were registered in the corresponding finger of the A and B brothers. The A and B groups are strictly homogeneous, consequently the frequency of their patterns in corresponding fingers ought to be alike. The success with which this test has been fulfilled in the present case, is passably good, its exact degree being shown in the following paragraphs, where the numbers of entries under each head are arranged in as orderly a manner as the case admits, the smaller of the two numbers being the one that stands first, whether it was an A or a B. All instances in which there were at least five entries under either A or B, are included; the rest being disregarded. The result is as follows—

I. Thirteen cases of more or less congruity between the number of A and B entries under the same head—5–7; 5–7; 5–8; 6–8; 7–10; 8–9; 8–12; 9–12; 10–10; 11–13; 12–16; 14–18; 72–73. (This last refers to loops on the middle finger.)

II. Six cases of more or less incongruity—1–7; 6–12; 14–20; 14–22; 22–35; 39–50.

The three Tables, XXIV., XXV., XXVI., contain the results of the tabulations and the deductions from them.

TABLE XXIV.

Comparison of three Fingers of the Right Hand in 150 Fraternal Couplets.

Index No. of Pattern.	Fore-fingers.			Middle fingers.			Ring-fingers.		
	Down columns.	Along lines.	Double events.	Down columns.	Along lines.	Double events.	Down columns.	Along lines.	Double events.
	A	B	A and B	A	B	A and B	A	B	A and B
1	15	12	4	8	5	2	7	5	1
2	3	2	...	3	2	...	...	...	...
6	2	2	1	...	...	...	2	4	...
7	...	2	...	2	1	...	7	5	1
8	...	...	...	...	...	...	...	1	...
9	1	7	...	4	1	1	7	1	...
12	1	...	...	2	...	...	...	...	...
13	...	...	...	2	1	...	...	...	...
14	4	3	...	4	4	1	20	14	1
15	16	12	3	4	2	...	3	4	...
16	2	3	...	2	3	...	10	7	2
17	4	3	...	3	...	...	...	...	...
18	...	...	...	4	1	...	18	14	6
19	3	3	...	2	5	...	1	...	...
20	...	...	...	...	...	...	1	3	1
21	...	1	...	...	...	...	...	...	...
22	...	4	...	1	8	...	1	2	...
23	1	...	...	1	...	...	6	...	...
27	1	...	...	...	...	...	...	...	...
32	1	...	...	1	3	...	4	4	...
33	3	1	1	1	...	...	3	3	1
34	3	2	...	4	1	...	...	...	...
35	2	3	...	...	5	...	9	12	2
38	2	1	...	...	...	...	...	...	...
39	4	...	...	3	1	...	...	...	...
40	13	11	1	14	22	6	9	8	...
41	12	8	...	1	3	...	...	1	...
42	22	35	5	73	72	35	39	50	16
43	10	10	3	4	1	...	...	3	...
44	2	1	...	...	2	...	...	2	...
45	1	1	...	...	...	...	...	...	...
46	8	6	1	3	1	...	...	1	...
47	3	4	...	...	...	...	...	...	...
48	6	12	1	4	6	...	2	3	...
49	1	1	...	...	...	...	...	...	...
52	...	...	...	...	...	...	1	...	...
53	...	...	...	...	...	...	...	1	...

TABLE XXV.

Comparison between Random and Observed Events.

Fore.		Middle.		Ring.	
Random.	Observed.	Random.	Observed.	Random.	Observed
1.20	4	0.26	2	0.23	1
0.08	...	0.11	1	0.05	...
1.28	3	0.05	...	0.23	
0.08	...	0.07	...	1.87	1
0.06	...	0.05	...	0.08	...
0.95	1	2.05	6	0.46	2
0.64	...	34.08	35	1.68	6
5.18	5	0.16	...	0.11	...
0.67	3			0.06	1
0.32	1			0.72	2
0.08	...			0.48	...
0.48	1			13.00	16
All others.					
0.29	2	0.28	1	0.12	1
11.31	20	37.11	45	19.09	30

TABLE XXVI.

Centesimal Scale (to nearest whole numbers).

150 fraternal couplets.	Random.	Observed.	Utmost Possibilities.	Reduced to lower limit = 0			Reduced to upper limit = 100.		
							Centesimal scale.		
Fore-finger	11.31	20	115	0	9	104	0°	9°	100°
Middle	37.11	45	117	0	10	80	0°	10°	100°
Ring	19.09	31	118	0	12	99	0°	12°	100°
				Mean			0°	10°	100°
50 additional couplets.									
Middle finger only ..	8.2	11	22	0	3	14	0°	21°	100°
Loops only, and on middle finger only.									
150 couplets	34.0	35	72	0	1	72	0°	1¼°	100°
50 couplets	6.4	7	14	0	0.6	8	0°	8°	100°

Table XXIV. contains all the Observed events, and is to be read thus, beginning at the first entry. Pattern No. 1 occurs on the right fore-finger fifteen times among the A brothers, and twelve times among the B brothers; while in four of these cases both brothers have that same pattern.

Table XXV. compares the Random events with the Observed ones. Every case in which the calculated expectation is equal to or exceeds 0.05, is inserted in detail; the remaining group of petty cases are summed together and their totals entered in the bottom line. For fear of misapprehension or forgetfulness, one other example of the way in which the Randoms are calculated will be given here, taking for the purpose the first entry in Table XXIV. Thus, the number of all the different combinations of the 150 A with the 150 B individuals in the 150 couplets, is 150 × 150. Out of these, the number of double events in which pattern No. 1 would appear in the same combination, is 15 × 12=180. Therefore in 150 trials, the double event of pattern No. 1 would appear upon the average, on 180 divided by 150, or on 1.20 occasions. As a matter of fact, it appeared four times. These figures will be found in the first line of Table XXV.; the rest of its contents have been calculated in the same way.

Leaving aside the Randoms that exceed 0 but are less than 1, there are nineteen cases in which the Random may be compared with the Observed values; in all but two of these the Observed are the highest, and in these two the Random exceed the Observed by only trifling amounts, namely, 5.18 Random against 5.00 Observed; 1.87 Random against 1.00 Observed. It is impossible, therefore, to doubt from the steady way in which the Observed values overtop the Randoms, that there is a greater average likeness in the finger marks of two brothers, than in those of two persons taken at hazard.

Table XXVI. gives the results of applying the centesimal scale to the measurement of the average closeness of fraternal resemblance, in respect to finger prints, according to the method and under the reservations already explained in page 120. The average value thus assigned to it is a little more than 10°. The values obtained from the three fingers severally, from which that average was derived, are 9°, 10°, and 12°; they agree together better than might have been expected. The value obtained from a set of fifty additional couplets of the middle fingers only, of fraternals, is wider, being 21°. Its inclusion with the rest raises the average of all to between 10 and 11.

In the pre-eminently frequent event of loops with an outward slope on the middle finger, it is remarkable that the Random cases are nearly equal to the Observed ones; they are 34.08 to 35.00. It was to obtain some assurance that this equality was not due to statistical accident, that the additional set of fifty couplets were tabulated. They tell, however, the same tale, viz., 6.4 Randoms to 7.0 Observed. The loops on the fore-fingers confirm this, showing 5.18 Randoms to 5.00 Observed; those on the ring-finger have the same peculiarity, though in a slighter degree, 13 to 16: the average of other patterns shows a much greater difference than that. I am unable to account for this curious behaviour of the loops, which can hardly be due to statistical accident, in the face of so much concurrent evidence.

Twins. The signs of heredity between brothers and sisters ought to be especially apparent between twins of the same sex, who are physiologically related in a peculiar degree and are sometimes extraordinarily alike. More rarely, they are remarkably dissimilar. The instances of only a moderate family resemblance between twins of the same sex are much less frequent than between ordinary brothers and sisters, or between twins of opposite sex. All this has been discussed in my *Human Faculty*. In order to test the truth of the expectation, I procured prints of the fore, middle, and ring-fingers of seventeen sets of twins, and compared them, with the results shown in Table XXVII.

The result is that out of the seventeen sets (= 51 couplets), two sets agree in all their three couplets of fingers; four sets agree in two; five sets agree in one of the couplets. There are instances of partial agreement in five others, and a disagreement throughout in only one of the seventeen sets. In another collection of seventeen sets, made to compare with this, six agreed in two of their three couplets, and five agreed in one of them. There cannot then be the slightest doubt as to the strong tendency to resemblance in the finger patterns in twins.

This remark must by no means be forced into the sense of meaning that the similarity is so great, that the finger print of one twin might occasionally be mistaken for that of the other. When patterns fall into the same class, their general forms may be conspicuously different (see p. 75), while their smaller details, namely, the number of ridges and the minutiæ, are practically independent of the pattern.

TABLE XXVII.

17 SETS OF TWINS (A and B).

Comparison between the patterns on the Fore, Middle, and Ring-fingers,
respectively, of the Right hand.

Agreement (=), 19 cases; partial (...), 13 cases ; disagreement (x), 19 cases.

	A B	A B	A B	A B	A B
Fore	42 = 42	21 = 21	40 = 40	6 = 6	1 = 1
Middle	42 = 42	8 = 8	32 × 42	15 ... 32	42 = 42
Ring	42 = 42	8 = 8	42 = 42	33 = 33	40 × 19
Fore	42 = 42	43 × 15	1 = 1	15 × 34	2 ... 42
Middle	42 = 42	42 ... 40	1 × 40	42 = 42	42 = 42
Ring	42 ... 46	35 = 35	40 ... 42	14 × 32	42 × 14
Fore	49 ... 14	15 × 49	15 ... 16	1 × 42	1 × 15
Middle	42 = 42	23 × 14	19 × 42	42 ... 48	32 × 22
Ring	9 ... 32	14 ... 16	6 ... 18	42 × 8	18 × 23
Fore	48 × 33	(loop) × 9			
Middle	42 × 22	48 × 22			
Ring	14 ... 6	9 ... 35			

It may be mentioned that I have an inquiry in view, which has not yet been fairly begun, owing to the want of sufficient data, namely to determine the minutest biological unit that may be hereditarily transmissible. The minutiæ in the finger prints of twins seem suitable objects for this purpose.

Children of like-patterned Parents. When two parents are alike, the average resemblance, in stature at all events, which their children bear to them, is as close as the fraternal resemblance between the children, and twice as close as that which the children bear to either parent separately, when the parents are unlike.

The fifty-eight parentages affording fifty couplets of the fore, middle, and ring-fingers respectively give 58 × 3 = 174 parental couplets in all; of these, 27 or 14 per cent are alike in their pattern, as shown by Table XXVIII. The total number of children to these twenty-seven pairs is 109, of which 59 (or 54 per cent) have the same pattern as their parents. This fact requires analysis, as on account of the great frequency of loops, and especially of the pattern No. 42 on the middle finger, a large number of the cases of similarity of pattern between child and parents would be mere random coincidences.

There are nineteen cases of both parents having the commonest of the loop patterns, No. 42, on a corresponding finger. They have between them seventy-five children, of whom forty-eight have the pattern No. 42, on the same finger as their parents, and eighteen others have loops of other kinds on that same finger, making a total of sixty-six coincidences out of the possible 75, or 88 per cent, which is a great increase upon the normal proportion of loops of the No. 42 pattern in the fore, middle, and ring-fingers collectively. Again, there are three cases of both parents having a tendrilled-loop No. 15, which ranks as a whorl. Out of their total number of seventeen children, eleven have whorls and only six have loops.

Lastly, there is a single case of both parents having an arch, and all their three children have arches; whereas in the total of 109 children in the table, there are only four other cases of an arch.

This partial analysis accounts for the whole of the like-patterned parents, except four couples, which are one of No. 34, two of No. 40, and one of No. 46. These concur in telling the same general tale, recollecting that No. 46 might almost be reckoned as a transitional case between a loop and a whorl.

The decided tendency to hereditary transmission cannot be gainsaid in the face of these results, but the number of cases is too few to justify quantitative conclusions. It is not for the present worth while to extend them, for the reason already mentioned, namely, an ignorance of the allowance that ought to be made for related patterns. On this account it does not seem useful to print the results of a large amount of tabulation bearing on the simple filial relationship between the child and either parent separately, except so far as appears in the following paragraph.

Relative Influence of the Father and the Mother. Through one of those statistical accidents which are equivalent to long runs of luck at a gaming table, a concurrence in the figures brought out by Mr. Collins suggested to him the existence of a decided preponderance of maternal influence in the hereditary transmission of finger patterns. His further inquiries have, however, cast some doubt on earlier and provisional conclusions, and the following epitomises all of value that can as yet be said in favour of the superiority of the maternal influence.

TABLE XXVIII. *Children of like-patterned Parents.*

The 27 cases.	Patterns of—	F.	M.	—of Sons.	Alike.	Total sons.	—of Daughters.	Alike.	Total daughters.	Total children.	Alike.
1	Fore	1	1	1	1	1	1, 1	2	2	3	3
2		34	34	34	1	1	42, 48	…	2	3	1
3		40	40	41	…	1	2, 40	1	2	3	1
4		42	42	48	…	1	42	1	1	2	1
5	Middle	40	40	40	1	1	40	1	1	2	2
6		42	42	42	1	1	…	…	…	1	1
7		42	42	42	1	1	40	…	1	2	1
8		42	42	42, 38, 42, 42	3	4	40, 1	…	2	6	3
9		42	42	42	1	1	40, 42	1	2	3	2
10		42	42	48, 48, 42, 14	1	4	42, 42, 48, 42, 42	4	5	9	5
11		42	42	42	1	1	1, 40	…	2	3	1
12		42	42	40	…	1	42, 42, 42, 42	4	4	5	4
13		42	42	1	…	1	…	…	…	1	…
14		42	42	42	1	1	42, 42, 42	3	3	4	4
15		42	42	42, 46, 42	2	3	42, 42, 42, 42, 42, 42, 42	7	7	10	9
16		42	42	34, 42	1	2	33, 42	1	2	4	2
17		42	42	42	1	1	40, 42, 1	1	3	4	2
18		42	42	…	…	…	42, 42 (twins)	2	2	2	2
19	Ring	14	14	33, 42, 14	1	3	32, 40	…	2	5	1
20		14	14	42, 16	…	2	16, 14, 42, 42	1	4	6	1
21		14	14	6	…	1	9, 35, 48, 32, 14	1	5	6	1
22		42	42	40	…	1	40	…	1	2	…
23		42	42	42, 42, 42	3	3	40, 42	1	2	5	4
24		42	42	…	…	…	40, 42	1	2	2	1
25		42	42	42, 42	2	2	42, 40, 42	2	3	5	4
26		42	42	49, 14	…	2	42, 42, 42	3	3	5	3
27		46	46	48, 40, 40, 16	…	4	16, 38	…	2	6	…
					22	44	Daughters ……	37	65	109	59
							Sons ……	22	44		
							Total Children …	59	109		

The fore, middle, and ring-fingers of the right hands of the father, mother, and all their accessible children, in many families, were severally tabulated under the fifty-three heads already specified. The total number of children was 389, namely, 136 sons and 219 daughters. The same pattern was found on the same finger, both of a child and of one or other of his parents, in the following number of cases—

TABLE XXIX.

Relative Influence of Father and Mother.

	Fore.	Middle.	Ring.	Totals.	Corrected Totals.	
Father and son ...	17	35	28	80	80	} 149
" " daughter	29	52	30	(111)	69	
Mother and son ..	18	50	26	94	94	} 186
" " daughter	38	75	35	(148)	94	

The entries in the first three columns are not comparable on equal terms, on account of the large difference between the numbers of the sons and daughters. This difference is easily remedied by multiplying the number of daughters by $^{136}/_{29}$, that is by 0.621, as has been done in the fifth column headed Corrected Totals. It would appear from these figures, that the maternal influence is more powerful than the paternal in the proportion of 186 to 149, or as 5 to 4; but, as some of the details from which the totals are built up, vary rather widely, it is better for the present to reserve an opinion as to their trustworthiness.

Chapter XII
Races and Classes

The races whose finger prints I have studied in considerable numbers are English, pure Welsh, Hebrew, and Negro; also some Basques from Cambo in the French Pyrenees, twenty miles south-east of Bayonne. For the Welsh prints I am primarily indebted to the very obliging help of Mr. R. W. Atkinson, of Cardiff, who interested the masters of schools in purely Welsh-speaking mountainous districts on my behalf; for the Hebrew prints to Mr. Isidore Spielman, who introduced me to the great Hebrew schools in London, whose head-masters gave cordial assistance; and for the Negro prints to Sir George Taubman Goldie, Dep. Governor of the Royal Niger Co., who interested Dr. Crosse on my behalf, from whom valuable sets of prints were received, together with particulars of the races of the men from whom they were made. As to the Basques, they were printed by myself.

It requires considerable patience and caution to arrive at trustworthy conclusions, but it may emphatically be said that there is no *peculiar* pattern which characterises persons of any of the above races. There is no particular pattern that is special to any one of them, which when met with enables us to assert, or even to suspect, the nationality of the person on whom it appeared. The only differences so far observed, are statistical, and cannot be determined except through patience and caution, and by discussing large groups.

I was misled at first by some accidental observations, and as it seemed reasonable to expect to find racial differences in finger marks, the inquiries were continued in varied ways until hard fact had made hope no longer justifiable.

After preliminary study, I handed over the collection of racial finger prints to Mr. F. Howard Collins, who kindly undertook the labour of tabulating them in many ways, of which it will be only necessary to give an example. Thus, at one time attention was concentrated on a single finger and a single pattern, the most instructive instance being that of arches on the right fore-finger. They admit of being defined with sufficient clearness, having only one doubtful frontier of much importance, namely that at which they begin to break away into nascent-loops, etc. They also occur with considerable frequency on the fore-finger, so the results from a few hundred specimens ought to be fairly trustworthy. It mattered little in the inquiry, at what level the limit was drawn to separate arches from nascent-loops, so long as the same limit was observed in all races alike. Much pains were taken to secure uniformity of treatment, and Mr. Collins selected two limits, the one based on a strict and the other on a somewhat less strict interpretation of the term "arches," but the latter was not so liberal as that which I had used myself in the earlier inquiries (see p. 111). His results showed no great difference in the proportionate frequency of arches in the different races, whichever limit was observed; the following table refers to the more liberal limit—

TABLE XXX.

Frequency of Arches in the Right Fore-Finger.

No. of Persons.	Race.	No. of Arches.	Per Cents.
250	English	34	13.6
250	Welsh	26	10.8
1332	Hebrew	105	7.9
250	Negro	27	11.3
	Hebrews in detail—		
500	Boys, Bell Lane School	35	7.0
400	Girls, Bell Lane School	34	8.5
220	Boys, Tavistock St. & Hanway St.	18	8.2
212	Girls, Hanway Street School	18	8.5

The two contrasted values here are the English and the Hebrew. The 1332 cases of the latter give a percentage result of 7.9, which differs as may be seen less than 1 per cent from that of any one of the four large groups upon which the average is based. The 250 cases of English are comparatively few, but the experience I have had of other English prints is so large as to enable me to say confidently that the percentage result of 13.6 is not too great. It follows, that the percentage of arches in the English and in the Hebrew differs in the ratio of 13.6 to 7.9, or nearly as 5 to 3. This is the largest statistical difference yet met with. The deficiency in arches among the Hebrews, and to some extent in loops also, is made up by a superiority in whorls, chiefly of the tendril or circlet-in-loop patterns.

It would be very rash to suppose that this relative infrequency of arches among the Hebrews was of fundamental importance, considering that such totally distinct races as the Welsh and the Negro have them in an intermediate proportion. Still, why does it occur? The only answer I can suggest is that the patterns being in some degree hereditary, such accidental preponderances as may have existed among a not very numerous ancestry might be perpetuated. I have some reason to believe that local peculiarities of this sort exist in England, the children in schools of some localities seeming to be statistically more alike in their patterns than English children generally.

Another of the many experiments was the tabulation separately by Mr. Collins of the fore, middle, and ring-fingers of the right hand of fifty persons of each of the five races above-mentioned: English, Welsh, Basque, Hebrew, and different groups of Negroes. The number of instances is of course too small for statistical deductions, but they served to make it clear that no very marked characteristic distinguished the races. The impressions from Negroes betray the general clumsiness of their fingers, but their patterns are not, so far as I can find, different from those of others, they are not simpler as judged either by their contours or by the number of origins, embranchments, islands, and enclosures contained in them. Still, whether it be from pure fancy on my part, or from the way in which they were printed, or from some real peculiarity, the general aspect of the Negro print strikes me as characteristic. The width of the ridges seems more uniform, their intervals more regular, and their courses more parallel than with us. In short, they give an idea of greater simplicity, due to causes that I have not yet succeeded in submitting to the test of measurement.

The above are only a few examples of the laborious work so kindly undertaken for me by Mr. F. H. Collins, but it would serve no useful purpose to give more in this book, as no positive results have as yet been derived from it other than the little already mentioned.

The most hopeful direction in which this inquiry admits of being pursued is among the Hill tribes of India, Australian blacks, and other diverse and so-called aboriginal races. The field of ethnology is large, and it would be unwise as yet to neglect the chance of somewhere finding characteristic patterns.

Differences between finger prints of different classes might continue to exist although those of different races are inconspicuous, because every race contains men of various temperaments and faculties, and we cannot tell, except by observation, whether any of these are correlated with the finger marks. Several different classes have been examined both by Mr. Collins and myself. The ordinary laboratory work supplies finger prints of persons of much culture, and of many students both in the Art and in the Science schools. I took a large number of prints from the worst idiots in the London district, through the obliging assistance of Dr. Fletcher Beech, of the Darenth Asylum; my collections made at Board Schools are numerous, and I have one of field labourers in Dorsetshire and Somersetshire. But there is no notable difference in any of them. For example; the measurements of the ridge-interval gave the same results in the art-students and in the science-students, and I have prints of eminent thinkers and of eminent statesmen that can be matched by those of congenital idiots.[1] No indications of temperament, character, or ability are to be found in finger marks, so far as I have been able to discover.

Of course these conclusions must not be applied to the general shape of the hand, which as yet I have not studied, but which seems to offer a very interesting field for exact inquiry.

---

1. The results arrived at by M. Féré in a Memoir (*Comptes Rendus, Soc. Biologie*, July 2, 1891; Masson, 120 Boulevard St. Germain, Paris) may be collated with mine. The Memoir is partly a review of my paper in the *Phil. Trans.*, and contains many observations of his own. His data are derived from epileptics and others mentally affected. He has, by the way, curiously misinterpreted my views about symmetry.

CHAPTER XIII
GENERA

The same familiar patterns recur in every large collection of finger prints, and the eye soon selects what appear to be typical forms; but are they truly "typical" or not? By a type I understand an ideal form around which the actual forms are grouped, very closely in its immediate neighbourhood, and becoming more rare with increasing rapidity at an increasing distance from it, just as is the case with shot marks to the right or left of a line drawn vertically through the bull's eye of a target. The analogy is exact; in both cases there is a well-defined point of departure; in both cases the departure of individual instances from that point is due to a multitude of independently variable causes. In short, both are realisations of the now well-known theoretical law of Frequency of Error. The problem then is this—take some one of the well-marked patterns, such as it appears on a particular digit,—say a loop on the right thumb; find the average number of ridges that cross a specified portion of it; then this average value will determine an ideal centre from which individual departures may be measured; next, tabulate the frequency of the departures that attain to each of many successive specified distances from that ideal centre; then see whether their diminishing frequency as the distances increase, is or is not in accordance with the law of frequency of error. If it is, then the central form has the attributes of a true type, and such will be shown to be the case with the loops of either thumb. I shall only give the data and the results, not the precise way in which they are worked out, because an account of the method employed in similar cases will be found in *Natural Inheritance*, and again in the Memoir on Finger Prints in the *Phil. Trans.*; it is too technical to be appropriate here, and would occupy too much space. The only point which need be briefly explained and of which nonmathematical readers might be ignorant, is how a single numerical table derived from abstract calculations can be made to apply to such minute objects as finger prints, as well as to the shot marks on a huge target; what is the common unit by which departures on such different scales are measured? The answer is that it is a self-contained unit appropriate to *each series severally*, and technically called the Probable Error, or more briefly, P.E., in the headings to the following tables. In order to determine it, the range of the central half of the series has to be measured, namely, of that part of the series which remains after its two extreme quarters have been cut off and removed. The series had no limitation before, its two ends tailing away indefinitely into nothingness, but, by the artifice of lopping off a definite fraction of the whole series from both ends of it, a sharply defined length, call it PQ, is obtained. Such series as have usually to be dealt with are fairly symmetrical, so the position of the half-way point M, between P and Q, corresponds with rough accuracy to the average of the positions of all the members of the series, that is to the point whence departures have to be measured. MP, or MQ,—or still better, ½ (MP + MQ) is the above-mentioned Probable Error. It is so called because the amount of Error, or Departure from M of any one observation, falls just as often within the distance PE as it falls without it. In the calculated tables of the Law of Frequency, PE (or a multiple of it) is taken as unity. In each observed

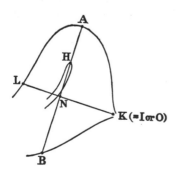

series, the actual measures have to be converted into another scale, in which the PE of that series is taken as unity. Then observation and calculation may be compared on equal terms.

Observations were made on the loops of the right and left thumbs, respectively. AHB is taken as the primary line of reference in the loop; it is the line that, coinciding with the axis of the *uppermost portion*, and that only, of the core, cuts the summit of the core at H, the upper outline at A, and the lower outline, if it cuts it at all, as it nearly always does, at B. K is the centre of the single triangular plot that appears in the loop, which may be either I or O. KNL is a perpendicular from K to the axis, cutting it at N, and the outline beyond at L. In some loops N will lie above H, as in Plate 4, Fig. 8; in some it may coincide with H. (See Plate 6 for numerous varieties of loop.) These points were pricked in each print with a fine needle; the print was then turned face downwards and careful measurements made between the prick holes at the back. Also the number of ridges in AH were counted, the ridge at A being reckoned as 0, the next ridge as 1, and so on up to H. Whenever the line AH passed across the neck of a bifurcation, there was necessarily a single ridge on one side of the point of' intersection and two ridges on the other, so there would clearly be doubt whether to reckon the neck as one or as two ridges. A compromise was made by counting it as 1½. After the number of ridges in AH had been counted in each case, any residual fractions of ½ were alternately treated as 0 and as 1. Finally, six series were obtained; three for the right thumb, and three for the left. They referred, respectively, (1) to the Number of Ridges in AH; (2) to $^{KL}/_{NB}$; (3) to $^{AN}/_{AH}$, all the three being independent of stature. The number of measures in each of the six series varied from 140 to 176; they are reduced to percentages in Table XXXI.

We see at a glance that the different numbers of ridges in AH do not occur with equal frequency, that a single ridge in the thumb is a rarity, and so are cases above fifteen in number, but those of seven, eight, and nine are frequent. There is clearly a rude order in their distribution, the number of cases tailing away into nothingness, at the top and bottom of the column. A vast amount of statistical analogy assures us that the orderliness of the distribution would be increased if many more cases had been observed, and later on, this inference will be confirmed. There is a sharp inferior limit to the numbers of ridges, because they cannot be less than 0, but independently of this, we notice the infrequency of small numbers as well as of large ones. There is no strict limit to the latter, but the trend of the entries shows that forty, say, or more ridges in AH are practically impossible. Therefore, in no individual case can the number of ridges in AH depart very widely from seven, eight, or nine, though the range of possible departures is not sharply defined, except at the lower limit of 0. The range of variation is *not* "rounded off," to use a common but very inaccurate expression often applied to the way in which genera are isolated. The range of possible departures is not defined by any rigid boundary, but the rarity of the stragglers rapidly increases with the distance at which they are found, until no more of them are met with.

The values of $^{KI}\!/_{NB}$ and of $^{AN}\!/_{AH}$ run in a less orderly sequence, but concur distinctly in telling a similar tale. Considering the paucity of the observations, there is nothing in these results to contradict the expectation of increased regularity, should a large addition be made to their number.

TABLE XXXI.

No. of ridges in AH.	No. of cases reduced to per cents. Right. (171 cases.)	Left. (166 cases.)	$\frac{KL}{NB}$	No. of cases reduced to per cents. Right. (149 cases.)	Left. (140 cases.)	$\frac{AN}{AH}$	No. of cases reduced to per cents. Right (176 cases.)	Left (163 cases.)
1	1	…	0.3–0.4	3	2	0.1–0.2	2	1
2	2	1	0.5–0.6	8	11	0.3–0.4	7	3
3	2	3	0.7–0.8	9	14	0.5–0.6	11	3
4	2	5	0.9–1.0	21	18	0.7–0.8	9	9
5	3	5	1.1–1.2	16	23	0.9–1.0	22	15
6	4	18	1.3–1.4	24	7	1.1–1.2	15	13
7	8	14	1.5–1.6	8	10	1.3–1.4	12	12
8	8	16	1.7–1.8	3	6	1.5–1.6	11	14
9	11	16	1.9–2.0	5	6	1.7–1.8	8	10
10	11	10	2.1–2.2	1	1	1.9–2.0	1	5
11	9	8	above	2	2	2.1–2.2	…	…
12	14	10				2.3–2.4	1	6
13	11	8				2.5–2.6	…	4
14	10	2				2.7–2.8	…	3
15	7	…				2.9–3.0	…	1
above	6	…				above.	1	1
	100	100		100	100		100	100

TABLE XXXII.

Ordinates to the six schemes of Distribution, being the ordinates drawn from the base of each scheme at selected centesimal divisions of the base.

Abscissae reckoned in centesimal parts of the interval between the limits of the scheme. 0° to 100°.	No. of ridges in AH.				Values of $\frac{KL}{NB}$				Values of $\frac{AN}{AH}$			
	Right.		Left.		Right.		Left.		Right.		Left.	
	Observed.	Calculated from M = 10.4 p.e. = 2.3	Observed.	Calculated from M = 7.8 p.e. = 1.9	Observed.	Calculated from M = 1.15 p.e. = 0.25	Observed.	Calculated from M = 1.10 p.e. = 0.31	Observed.	Calculated from M = 1.08 p.e. = 0.30	Observed.	Calculated from M = 1.36 p.e. = 0.36
5	3.8	4.8	3.8	3.2	0.54	0.54	0.49	0.35	0.36	0.32	0.58	0.48
10	5.5	6.0	4.8	4.2	0.64	0.67	0.59	0.51	0.50	0.48	0.74	0.68
20	7.3	7.5	5.8	5.4	0.85	0.84	0.78	0.71	0.66	0.67	0.96	0.91
25	7.9	8.1	6.1	5.9	0.91	0.90	0.83	0.79	0.79	0.75	1.00	1.00
30	8.5	8.6	6.4	6.3	0.99	0.95	0.89	0.86	0.87	0.82	1.04	1.08
40	9.5	9.5	7.1	7.4	1.05	1.05	1.00	0.98	0.98	0.93	1.21	1.22
50	10.5	10.4	7.8	7.8	1.15	1.15	1.10	1.10	1.04	1.05	1.37	1.36
60	11.3	11.3	8.4	8.2	1.29	1.25	1.18	1.22	1.18	1.17	1.48	1.50
70	12.1	12.2	9.3	9.3	1.33	1.35	1.32	1.34	1.31	1.28	1.66	1.64
75	12.5	12.7	9.9	9.7	1.41	1.40	1.46	1.41	1.39	1.35	1.73	1.72
80	13.0	13.3	11.0	10.2	1.45	1.46	1.53	1.49	1.48	1.43	1.90	2.81
90	14.3	14.8	11.5	11.4	1.77	1.63	1.73	1.69	1.69	1.62	2.23	2.04
95	15.0	16.0	12.2	12.2	2.00	1.76	1.80	1.85	1.81	1.78	2.48	2.24

TABLE XXXIII.

Ordinates to the six curves of distribution, drawn from the axis of each curve at selected centesimal divisions of it. They are here reduced to a common measure, by dividing the observed deviations in each series by the probable error appropriate to the series, and multiplying by 100. For the values of M, whence the deviations are measured, and for those of the corresponding probable error, see the heading to the columns in Table II.

Abscissae reckoned in centesimal parts of the interval between the limits of the curve. 0° to 100°.	No. of Ridges in AH.		Values of $\frac{KL}{NB}$		Values of $\frac{AN}{AH}$		Observed. Mean of the corresponding ordinates in the six curves after reduction to the common scale of p.e.=100.965 observations in all.	Calculated. Ordinates to the normal curve of distribution, probable error=100.
	Right.	Left.	Right.	Left.	Right.	Left.		
5	−291	−211	−244	−196	−230	−217	−251	−244
10	−213	−158	−204	−164	−183	−172	−182	−190
20	−135	−105	−120	−103	−130	−111	−117	−125
(P) 25	−109	− 84	− 92	− 87	− 87	−100	− 93	−100
30	− 83	− 74	− 64	− 68	− 60	− 89	− 73	− 78
40	− 44	− 37	− 44	− 31	− 23	− 42	− 37	− 38
(M) 50	+ 4	0	0	0	0	0	+ 1	0
60	+ 39	+ 31	+ 56	+ 23	+ 43	+ 33	+ 38	+ 38
70	+ 74	+ 79	+ 72	+ 68	+ 87	+ 83	+ 77	+ 78
(Q) 75	+ 91	+ 116	+104	+116	+113	+103	+107	+100
80	+ 113	+ 168	+120	+138	+143	+150	+139	+125
90	+ 170	+200	+248	+203	+213	+242	+213	+190
95	+200	+231	+340	+225	+253	+311	+260	+244

Table XXXII. is derived from Table XXXI. by a process described by myself in many publications, more especially in *Natural Inheritance*, and will now be assumed as understood. Each of the six pairs of columns contain, side by side, the Observed and Calculated values of one of the six series, the data on which the calculations were made being also entered at the top. The calculated figures agree with the observed ones very respectably throughout, as can be judged even by those who are ignorant of the principles of the method. Let us take the value that 10 per cent of each of the six series falls short of, and 90 per cent exceed; they are entered in the line opposite 10; we find for the six pairs successively,

Obs.: 5.5   4.8   0.64   0.59   0.50   0.74

Calc.: 6.0   4.2   0.67   0.51   0.48   0.68

The correspondence between the more mediocre cases is much closer than these, and very much closer than between the extreme cases given in the table, namely, the values that 5 per cent fall short of, and 95 exceed. These are of course less regular, the observed instances being very few; but even here the observations are found to agree respectably well with the proportions given by calculation, which is necessarily based upon the supposition of an infinite number of cases having been included in the series.

As the want of agreement between calculation and observation must be caused in part by the paucity of observations, it is worth while to make a larger group, by throwing the six series together, as in Table XXXIII., making a grand total of 965 observations. Their value is not so great as if they were observations taken from that number of different persons, still they are equivalent to a large increase of those already discussed. The six series of observed values were made comparable on equal terms by first reducing them to a uniform PE and then by assigning to M, the point of departure, the value of 0. The results are given in the last column but one, where the orderly run of the observed data is much more conspicuous than it was before. Though there is an obvious want of exact symmetry in the observed values, their general accord with those of the calculated values is very fair. It is quite close enough to establish the general proposition, that we are justified in the conception of a typical form of loop, different for the two thumbs; the departure from the typical form being usually small, sometimes rather greater, and rarely greater still.

I do not see my way to discuss the variations of the arches, because they possess no distinct points of reference. But their general appearance does not give the impression of clustering around a typical centre. They suggest the idea of a fountain-head, whose stream begins to broaden out from the first.

As regards other patterns, I have made many measurements altogether, but the specimens of each sort were comparatively few, except in whorled patterns. In all cases where I was able to form a well-founded opinion, the existence of a typical centre was indicated.

It would be tedious to enumerate the many different trials made for my own satisfaction, to gain assurance that the variability of the several patterns is really of the quasi-normal kind just described. In the first trial I measured in various ways the dimensions of about 500 enlarged photographs of loops, and about as many of other patterns, and found that the measurements in each and every case formed a quasi-normal series. I do not care to submit these results, because they necessitate more explanation and analysis than the interest of the corrected results would perhaps justify, to eliminate from them the effect of variety of size of thumb, and some other uncertainties. Those measurements referred to some children, a few women, many youths, and a fair number of adults; and allowance has to be made for variability in stature in each of these classes.

The proportions of a typical loop on the thumb are easily ascertained if we may assume that the most frequent values of its variable elements, taken separately, are the same as those that enter into the most frequent combination of the elements taken collectively. This would necessarily be true if the variability of each element separately, and that of the sum of them in combination, were all strictly normal, but as they are only quasi-normal, the assumption must be tested. I have done so by making the comparisons (A) and (B) shown in Table XXXIV., which come out correctly to within the first decimal place.

TABLE XXXIV.

	Right Thumb.	Left Thumb.
(a) Median of all the values of KL ..	12.5	10.1
(b) Median of all the values of NB ..	10.1	8.9
(A) Value of a/b.	1.24	1.11
(A) Median of all the fractions $^{KL}/_{NB}$ ..	1.15	1.10
(c) Median of all the values of AN ..	4.6	4.6
(d) Median of all the values of AH ..	4.4	3.3
(B) Value of c/d	1.05	1.40
(B) Median of all the fractions $^{AN}/_{AH}$ ..	1.08	1.36

It has been shown that the patterns are hereditary, and we have seen that they are uncorrelated with race or temperament or any other noticeable peculiarity, inasmuch as groups of very different classes are alike in their finger marks. They cannot exercise the slightest influence on marriage selection, the very existence both of the ridges and of the patterns having been almost overlooked; they are too small to attract attention, or to be thought worthy of notice. We therefore possess a perfect instance of promiscuity in marriage, or, as it is now called, panmixia, in respect to these patterns. We might consequently have expected them to be hybridised. But that is not the case; *they refuse to blend*. Their classes are as clearly separated as those of any of the genera of plants and animals. They keep pure and distinct, as if they had severally descended from a thorough-bred ancestry, each in respect to its own peculiar character.

As regards other forms of natural selection, we know that races are kept pure by the much more frequent destruction of those individuals who depart the more widely from the typical centre. But natural selection was shown to be inoperative in respect to individual varieties of patterns, and unable to exercise the slightest check upon their vagaries. Yet, for all that, the loops and other classes of patterns are isolated from one another just as thoroughly and just in the same way as are the genera or species of plants and animals. There is no statistical difference between the form of the law of distribution of individual Loops about their respective typical centres, and that of the law by which, say, the Shrimps described in Mr. Weldon's recent memoirs (*Proc. Roy. Soc.*, 1891 and 1892) are distributed about theirs. In both cases the distribution is in quasi-accordance with the theoretical law of Frequency of Error, this form of distribution being entirely caused in the patterns, by *internal* conditions, and in no way by natural selection in the ordinary sense of that term.

It is impossible not to recognise the fact so clearly illustrated by these patterns in the thumbs, that natural selection has no monopoly of influence in the construction of genera, but that it could be wholly dispensed with, the internal conditions acting by themselves being sufficient. When the internal conditions are in harmony with the external ones, as they appear to be in all long-established races, their joint effects will curb individual variability more tightly than either could do by itself. The normal character of the distribution about the typical centre will not be thereby interfered with. The probable divergence (= probable error) of an individual taken at random, will be lessened, and that is all.

Not only is it impossible to substantiate a claim for natural selection, that it is the sole agent in forming genera, but it seems, from the experience of artificial selection, that it is scarcely competent to do so by favouring mere *varieties*, in the sense in which I understand the term.

My contention is that it acts by favouring small *sports*. Mere varieties from a common typical centre blend freely in the offspring, and the offspring of every race whose *statistical* characters are constant, necessarily tend, as I have often shown, to regress towards their common typical centre. Sports, on the other hand, do not blend freely; they are fresh typical centres or sub-species, which suddenly arise we do not yet know precisely through what uncommon concurrence of circumstance, and which observations show to be strongly transmissible by inheritance.

A mere variety can never establish a sticking-point in the forward course of evolution, but each new sport affords one. A substantial change of type is effected, as I conceive, by a succession of small changes of typical centre, each more or less stable, and each being in its turn favoured and established by natural selection, to the exclusion of its competitors. The distinction between a mere variety and a sport is real and fundamental. I argued this point in *Natural Inheritance*, but had then to draw my illustrations from non-physiological experiences, no appropriate physiological ones being then at hand: this want is now excellently supplied by observations of the patterns on the digits.

INDEX

GREAT MINDS PAPERBACK SERIES

ART

❏ Leonardo da Vinci—*A Treatise on Painting*

CRITICAL ESSAYS

❏ Desiderius Erasmus—*The Praise of Folly*
❏ Jonathan Swift—*A Modest Proposal and Other Satires*
❏ H. G. Wells—*The Conquest of Time*

ECONOMICS

❏ Charlotte Perkins Gilman—*Women and Economics:*
    A Study of the Economic Relation between Women and Men
❏ John Maynard Keynes—*The End of Laissez-Faire* and
    The Economic Consequences of the Peace
❏ John Maynard Keynes—*The General Theory of Employment, Interest, and Money*
❏ John Maynard Keynes—*A Tract on Monetary Reform*
❏ Thomas R. Malthus—*An Essay on the Principle of Population*
❏ Alfred Marshall—*Money, Credit, and Commerce*
❏ Alfred Marshall—*Principles of Economics*
❏ Karl Marx—*Theories of Surplus Value*
❏ John Stuart Mill—*Principles of Political Economy*
❏ David Ricardo—*Principles of Political Economy and Taxation*
❏ Adam Smith—*Wealth of Nations*
❏ Thorstein Veblen—*Theory of the Leisure Class*

HISTORY

❏ Edward Gibbon—*On Christianity*
❏ Alexander Hamilton, John Jay, and James Madison—*The Federalist*
❏ Herodotus—*The History*
❏ Thucydides—*History of the Peloponnesian War*
❏ Andrew D. White—*A History of the Warfare of Science with Theology*
    in Christendom

LAW

❏ John Austin—*The Province of Jurisprudence Determined*

POLITICS

❏ Walter Lippmann—*A Preface to Politics*

PSYCHOLOGY

❏ Sigmund Freud—*Totem and Taboo*

RELIGION

❏ Thomas Henry Huxley—*Agnosticism and Christianity and Other Essays*
❏ Ernest Renan—*The Life of Jesus*
❏ Upton Sinclair—*The Profits of Religion*
❏ Elizabeth Cady Stanton—*The Woman's Bible*
❏ Voltaire—*A Treatise on Toleration and Other Essays*

SCIENCE

❏ Jacob Bronowski—*The Identity of Man*

- ❏ Nicolaus Copernicus—*On the Revolutions of Heavenly Spheres*
- ❏ Francis Crick—*Of Molecules and Men*
- ❏ Marie Curie—*Radioactive Substances*
- ❏ Charles Darwin—*The Autobiography of Charles Darwin*
- ❏ Charles Darwin—*The Descent of Man*
- ❏ Charles Darwin—*The Origin of Species*
- ❏ Charles Darwin—*The Voyage of the* Beagle
- ❏ René Descartes—*Treatise of Man*
- ❏ Albert Einstein—*Relativity*
- ❏ Michael Faraday—*The Forces of Matter*
- ❏ Galileo Galilei—*Dialogues Concerning Two New Sciences*
- ❏ Francis Galton—*Finger Prints*
- ❏ Francis Galton—*Hereditary Genius*
- ❏ Ernst Haeckel—*The Riddle of the Universe*
- ❏ William Harvey—*On the Motion of the Heart and Blood in Animals*
- ❏ Werner Heisenberg—*Physics and Philosophy:*
  The Revolution in Modern Science
- ❏ Fred Hoyle—*Of Men and Galaxies*
- ❏ Julian Huxley—*Evolutionary Humanism*
- ❏ Thomas H. Huxley—*Evolution and Ethics* and *Science and Morals*
- ❏ Edward Jenner—*Vaccination against Smallpox*
- ❏ Johannes Kepler—*Epitome of Copernican Astronomy* and *Harmonies of the World*
- ❏ Charles Mackay—*Extraordinary Popular Delusions and the Madness of Crowds*
- ❏ James Clerk Maxwell—*Matter and Motion*
- ❏ Isaac Newton—*Opticks, Or Treatise of the Reflections, Inflections, and*
  Colours of Light
- ❏ Isaac Newton—*The Principia*
- ❏ Louis Pasteur and Joseph Lister—*Germ Theory and Its Application to Medicine* and *On the*
  Antiseptic Principle of the Practice of Surgery
- ❏ Moritz Schlick—*Space and Time in Contemporary Physics*
- ❏ William Thomson (Lord Kelvin) and Peter Guthrie Tait—
  The Elements of Natural Philosophy
- ❏ Alfred Russel Wallace—*Island Life*

SOCIOLOGY

- ❏ Emile Durkheim—*Ethics and the Sociology of Morals*

GREAT BOOKS IN PHILOSOPHY PAPERBACK SERIES

ESTHETICS

- ❏ Aristotle—*The Poetics*
- ❏ Aristotle—*Treatise on Rhetoric*

ETHICS

- ❏ Aristotle—*The Nicomachean Ethics*
- ❏ Marcus Aurelius—*Meditations*
- ❏ Jeremy Bentham—*The Principles of Morals and Legislation*
- ❏ John Dewey—*Human Nature and Conduct*
- ❏ John Dewey—*The Moral Writings of John Dewey, Revised Edition*
- ❏ Epictetus—*Enchiridion*
- ❏ David Hume—*An Enquiry Concerning the Principles of Morals*
- ❏ Immanuel Kant—*Fundamental Principles of the Metaphysic of Morals*
- ❏ John Stuart Mill—*Utilitarianism*
- ❏ George Edward Moore—*Principia Ethica*
- ❏ Friedrich Nietzsche—*Beyond Good and Evil*

- ❏ Plato—*Protagoras, Philebus,* and *Gorgias*
- ❏ Bertrand Russell—*Bertrand Russell On Ethics, Sex, and Marriage*
- ❏ Arthur Schopenhauer—*The Wisdom of Life* and *Counsels and Maxims*
- ❏ Adam Smith—*The Theory of Moral Sentiments*
- ❏ Benedict de Spinoza—*Ethics* and *The Improvement of the Understanding*

LOGIC

- ❏ George Boole—*The Laws of Thought*

METAPHYSICS/EPISTEMOLOGY

- ❏ Aristotle—*De Anima*
- ❏ Aristotle—*The Metaphysics*
- ❏ Francis Bacon—*Essays*
- ❏ George Berkeley—*Three Dialogues Between Hylas and Philonous*
- ❏ W. K. Clifford—*The Ethics of Belief and Other Essays*
- ❏ René Descartes—*Discourse on Method* and *The Meditations*
- ❏ John Dewey—*How We Think*
- ❏ John Dewey—*The Influence of Darwin on Philosophy and Other Essays*
- ❏ Epicurus—*The Essential Epicurus: Letters, Principal Doctrines, Vatican Sayings, and Fragments*
- ❏ Sidney Hook—*The Quest for Being*
- ❏ David Hume—*An Enquiry Concerning Human Understanding*
- ❏ David Hume—*Treatise of Human Nature*
- ❏ William James—*The Meaning of Truth*
- ❏ William James—*Pragmatism*
- ❏ Immanuel Kant—*The Critique of Judgment*
- ❏ Immanuel Kant—*Critique of Practical Reason*
- ❏ Immanuel Kant—*Critique of Pure Reason*
- ❏ Gottfried Wilhelm Leibniz—*Discourse on Metaphysics* and the *Monadology*
- ❏ John Locke—*An Essay Concerning Human Understanding*
- ❏ George Herbert Mead—*The Philosophy of the Present*
- ❏ Michel de Montaigne—*Essays*
- ❏ Charles S. Peirce—*The Essential Writings*
- ❏ Plato—*The Euthyphro, Apology, Crito,* and *Phaedo*
- ❏ Plato—*Lysis, Phaedrus,* and *Symposium*
- ❏ Bertrand Russell—*The Problems of Philosophy*
- ❏ George Santayana—*The Life of Reason*
- ❏ Arthur Schopenhauer—*On the Principle of Sufficient Reason*
- ❏ Sextus Empiricus—*Outlines of Pyrrhonism*
- ❏ Ludwig Wittgenstein—*Wittgenstein's Lectures: Cambridge, 1932–1935*
- ❏ Alfred North Whitehead—*The Concept of Nature*

PHILOSOPHY OF RELIGION

- ❏ Jeremy Bentham—*The Influence of Natural Religion on the Temporal Happiness of Mankind*
- ❏ Marcus Tullius Cicero—*The Nature of the Gods* and *On Divination*
- ❏ Ludwig Feuerbach—*The Essence of Christianity* and *The Essence of Religion*
- ❏ Paul Henry Thiry, Baron d'Holbach—*Good Sense*
- ❏ David Hume—*Dialogues Concerning Natural Religion*
- ❏ William James—*The Varieties of Religious Experience*
- ❏ John Locke—*A Letter Concerning Toleration*
- ❏ Lucretius—*On the Nature of Things*
- ❏ John Stuart Mill—*Three Essays on Religion*
- ❏ Friedrich Nietzsche—*The Antichrist*
- ❏ Thomas Paine—*The Age of Reason*
- ❏ Bertrand Russell—*Bertrand Russell On God and Religion*

SOCIAL AND POLITICAL PHILOSOPHY

- ❑ Aristotle—*The Politics*
- ❑ Mikhail Bakunin—*The Basic Bakunin: Writings, 1869–1871*
- ❑ Edmund Burke—*Reflections on the Revolution in France*
- ❑ John Dewey—*Freedom and Culture*
- ❑ John Dewey—*Individualism Old and New*
- ❑ John Dewey—*Liberalism and Social Action*
- ❑ G. W. F. Hegel—*The Philosophy of History*
- ❑ G. W. F. Hegel—*Philosophy of Right*
- ❑ Thomas Hobbes—*The Leviathan*
- ❑ Sidney Hook—*Paradoxes of Freedom*
- ❑ Sidney Hook—*Reason, Social Myths, and Democracy*
- ❑ John Locke—*Second Treatise on Civil Government*
- ❑ Niccolo Machiavelli—*The Prince*
- ❑ Karl Marx (with Friedrich Engels)—*The German Ideology*, including *Theses on Feuerbach and Introduction to the Critique of Political Economy*
- ❑ Karl Marx—*The Poverty of Philosophy*
- ❑ Karl Marx/Friedrich Engels—*The Economic and Philosophic Manuscripts of 1844* and *The Communist Manifesto*
- ❑ John Stuart Mill—*Considerations on Representative Government*
- ❑ John Stuart Mill—*On Liberty*
- ❑ John Stuart Mill—*On Socialism*
- ❑ John Stuart Mill—*The Subjection of Women*
- ❑ Montesquieu, Charles de Secondat—*The Spirit of Laws*
- ❑ Friedrich Nietzsche—*Thus Spake Zarathustra*
- ❑ Thomas Paine—*Common Sense*
- ❑ Thomas Paine—*Rights of Man*
- ❑ Plato—*Laws*
- ❑ Plato—*The Republic*
- ❑ Jean-Jacques Rousseau—*Émile*
- ❑ Jean-Jacques Rousseau—*The Social Contract*
- ❑ Bertrand Russell—*Political Ideas*
- ❑ Mary Wollstonecraft—*A Vindication of the Rights of Men*
- ❑ Mary Wollstonecraft—*A Vindication of the Rights of Women*